EARNING MONEY
AT HOME

a Consumer Publication

edited by   Edith Rudinger

published by   Consumers' Association
publishers of **Which?**

*illustrations
and cover by*   Mary Seymour

Which? Books are commissioned and researched
by the Association for Consumer Research
and published by Consumers' Association,
2 Marylebone Road, London NW1 4DX and
Hodder annd Stoughton , 47 Bedford Square,
London WC1B 3DP

ISBN 0 340 39961 0
and   0 85202 337 5

Photoset by Paston Press, Loddon, Norfolk
Printed by Hazell Watson & Viney Limited

Earning money at home

a Consumer Publication

Consumers' Association
publishers of **Which?**
2 Marylebone Road
London NW1 4DX

CONTENTS

WORKING AT HOME

There are practical advantages to working at home. You do not have to travel to work (although you may have to travel to get or dispose of your goods) so you have more time available, do not have to pay fares, go out in all weathers or worry about getting back by a certain time to collect children.

When working at home, you do not need to wear 'good' clothes (although you may need to have one respectable outfit for when you go to see people about work) or have your hair done or shave. You can be in for the plumber and when the meter reader calls, and be there to take parcels from the postman.

You are your own boss and can fit in your work at times to suit you and your clients—when the children or other members of the household are out during the day, or during the evening.

No one is going to stand over you and tell you what to do in detail. For some people, this is the main attraction of working on their own. But if you have been used to receiving instructions, you may find it is difficult at first to organise your own work, decide how long you can afford to spend on each item and make sure that you get it done. You may of necessity have to work late in the evenings even if you are tired or would like to watch television.

One of the disadvantages of working at home is that the work is always there, staring at you and reproaching you for not getting on with it while you are doing other things. And for someone who has been accustomed to going out to work, a disadvantage is lack of company while working, or even travelling.

You have to be better organised to work at home than if you are going out to work. The work itself may take up space in the house and make the place untidy. The most important thing is to keep everything to do with your work entirely separate from other things around you at home. If you are at work in a place away from home, you can leave everything on your desk or bench at the end of the day, knowing that it will be there waiting for you the next morning. This is unlikely to be easy when you are working at home, especially if there are children about. Unless you have a separate room, you have to make sure that all work, tools and materials can be put away and kept somewhere when you are not using them. It is particularly important not to get work money mixed up with domestic money.

It requires a great deal of self-discipline to work at home: in many ways, it is much easier to go out to work, leaving household jobs undone and unseen behind you, than it is to stay and have to work with distractions around. When you are at home and your attention wanders from your work, it is only too easy to justify doing some domestic task like going to hang out the washing or mow the lawn, just because the sun is shining.

motives

Why you want to start working at home is a question you should ask yourself before embarking on any job, if only to make sure that you do want to work and that you do not set out to do something that you cannot do effectively.

Will your earnings be an essential part of the family budget? Do you need the money solely to keep up with the effects of inflation, or as pocket money—a useful but not essential addition to the family income? These factors will affect what you do, when you do it, how you prepare for doing it (including any refresher course you may take), how many hours you spend on it, and how desperate you feel about taking whatever work you can.

For a retired person or an under-occupied housewife perhaps earning money may not be the primary consideration. But a second breadwinner's earnings which start off as pin money can end up as something the family relies on to pay the gas/garage/ holiday bill. If the money you earn is likely to become essential, you should not undertake work that is only seasonal or spasmodic unless this is the only way you can get started.

Your financial needs and motives play a paramount part in what you can afford to do and how long you can wait before breaking even or making a profit (however small). For some types of work, you would need some capital to begin with—for buying equipment, adapting your premises, getting in supplies or stock. And with some occupations, there is no likelihood of getting a cash return for quite some time after your investment.

what can you do?

Maybe there is an opportunity to convert an interest into a job or profession, or a hobby into a money-earning activity that gives you more satisfaction than conventional employment. A number of occupations can be carried out at home on a freelance basis, which may suit you better than doing the same work as an employee.

The advantage of starting off via a hobby is that you are doing the same thing that you have done for some time and feel confident about, with the added bonus that people are paying you for it. If you are thinking of doing this, you might benefit from some form of training, if you can afford the time and fees, to increase your knowledge, efficiency and skill.

Whatever you choose to do, it is important that it is something that is going to suit you. If you take up something unsuitable, for whatever reason, you are not going to like doing it and probably will not manage to do it properly. This may undermine your self-confidence and prevent you from doing something else that you could do well.

A woman who has been running a home and looking after children should realise that she has gained experience in decision-making and organisation, which she can now make use of.

Do not take up anything that is obviously too demanding, with which you may not be able to cope. Look at yourself objectively and decide what you are capable of. Your state of health is obviously important: there is no point in taking up work which will prove too much for you physically. An activity which involves a lot of standing or lifting and carrying may be too tiring for you; a lot of close work may prove a strain on middle-aged eyes; having to go out whatever the weather may be a risk to the health of an older person.

It is no good taking up work where you have to deal mainly with figures if you are not really good at them, since figurework is unlikely to grow on you. If you are more interested in people, choose the type of work where you would have the chance to meet people and deal with them and their requirements. Maybe you prefer practical to intellectual activity. How mobile are you? For some work, you must be able to go out occasionally, and may need a car.

How much time you have to spare or can squeeze out of the day for your work may be the crux of the decision on what you do. If you cannot work full-time without upsetting the family, you will have to find something that takes only part of your time. A mother with pre-school children will have to do her money-earning work in the evenings and at nights.

family and friends

You should discuss with your family what change your working at home is going to make to their lives. They may dislike the idea at first, but should know the reasons why you are doing it so that they can accept it without too much fuss.

Unless a husband or wife is in favour of the other spouse's working at home and is willing to give active support, things are going to be difficult. There are bound to be times when the other is going to have to do jobs he or she has not done in the past, as well as possibly giving some help in connection with the new work. Without support, it will be hard to work at home full-time, and even part-time could be complicated.

If you have elderly relatives or neighbours who depend on you in some way, try not to let them feel neglected, but explain to them that you are not going to be available as much as before, and that you may have to visit them at different times.

A major problem is dealing with casual visitors or social telephone calls during the hours that you have set aside for work. You need to be ruthless here, inviting them to call back at some other time when you can be free. It is no use thinking to yourself 'Oh, I'll make up the time later'—that time never comes, and you will have lost valuable working hours.

domestic duties

A housewife will have to organise her domestic life more carefully than before, whether she is the new earner at home or another member of the family now is.

shopping and cooking

You may have to keep bigger stocks of food and household supplies and always have something in reserve so that you do not have to interrupt your work to slip round to the shop for forgotten items.

You should not waste your precious time going round the shops looking for bargains; it may be more economic to use the time for earning more money. You may have to restrict yourself to a few shops which you know have the range of goods you want at reasonable prices. This would make it easier for other people (the children, perhaps) to do your shopping for you.

Buying in larger quantities can save time, even though it means that you are spending a lot of your newly-earned money all at one go—on a dozen tins, say, of baked beans or of cat food. If you do not have the time or means of transport to go to a special shop which sells in bulk, you could buy large quantities of any item you regularly need when it is on special offer at your local supermarket. Some supermarkets also sell a range of groceries in catering packs or multiple packs.

Having a freezer saves on shopping time because you can buy quantities of frozen food and vegetables to put in your freezer for when you need them. Also, you can cook a batch of dishes in advance and store them away in the freezer; this saves on cooking time, and avoids the cost of buying convenience foods for quick meals.

Time and money spent organising other people to get your home running smoothly is time well spent. If at the end of a rewarding working day you shut the door on your work only to step into a mucky kitchen, and face a pile of washing, no food in the 'fridge and a dejected household, all the pleasure in your work can evaporate.

If you are earning, you may be able to afford to have someone do some cooking for you in her home. Anyone tied to home who is a good cook may be glad of some extra money. Pay the proper rates. You could commission fruit pies or cakes from one, say, and stews or meat loaf from another, and you will have home cooking and a well-fed family, grateful friends and neighbours — and more time to follow your money-earning activities, with a clear conscience.

housework and garden
You may have to learn to be less perfectionist about the housework, and so will your family.

Where a man who had previously been out during the day now works at home, the woman who does the cleaning may have to rearrange the daily routine so as not to interfere with or distract him at work.

If you have not had many labour-saving appliances up to now, this may be the time to buy some. A good vacuum cleaner is going to get your carpets clean more quickly and efficiently than an old carpet sweeper. If you can afford a dishwasher, it may save much time and effort. An automatic washing machine, which carries out the whole washing process, including drying, without any help from you, will save your time if you can afford the initial capital expenditure.

Clothes which do not require hand washing or ironing can save time and energy: check the information label on clothes, sheets, pillowcases and duvet covers before you buy, to find out whether you can machine-wash and drip-dry them.

The garden can be a distraction for someone working at home. Consider converting part of the garden into relatively trouble-free lawn and shrubs so as to cut down on work; the rest of the family should take their turn.

It is important that husband, wife and children should be prepared to accept specific responsibilities. They will have to be willing to do more for themselves — help in the house, go shopping, take more responsibility for their clothes, belongings, and so on. If, for instance, teenage children are made responsible for looking after their clothes and making their beds, they will have to learn that if they do not do so there will be only dirty clothes to wear and unmade beds to sleep in. Do not give in and do it yourself for the sake of peace and tidiness.

time off
However well-meaning the rest of the family, it is likely that the mother will have to do a lot of overtime on the domestic front and even the best organised person will sometimes feel very tired.

Since you are your own best asset, do not exhaust yourself and your abilities by overwork. Make sure you give yourself some time off—evenings or week-ends and holidays. The flexibility of freelance work is one of its attractions, but it can be a hazard if it leads you to abuse your own resources. If earning money at home means ceaseless work, it will do you no good.

To avoid a feeling of isolation as you work at home, you can subscribe to *Homing-in*, a bi-monthly newsletter for homebased workers. As well as interchange of experiences through letters and articles, the newsletter has practical information and advice on problem areas, such as planning applications and enforcement notices, and offers the chance of contacting other homebased workers in the same area. The subscription is £15 a year, which includes a free advert in the newsletter if wished and a selected book service by mail; a contact list for members, circulated twice a year, is an optional extra at £2. For further details, contact Chris Oliver, 56 London Road, Milborne Port, Sherborne, Dorset DT9 5DW.

use of your house

Trouble with neighbours is obviously something you do not want. From the start, take particular care to tell them what you are doing and assure them that you will not bother them with your work as far as is possible.

Avoid noise at unreasonable times—no one will want to hear you typing or machining at 2 am, even though you may have an urgent order to finish.

Be particularly careful about visitors. People get annoyed by a constant stream of cars calling next door, parking in front of the wrong house, obstructing their entrance, callers shouting good-bye. To avoid friction here, ask your visitors and clients to cooperate and, for instance, to avoid walking over bits of other people's gardens.

If you live in a block of flats or on a housing estate, anything that needs a lot of storage space may not be possible. Stocks of plastic materials would be a fire risk and so would flammable liquids such as adhesives and solvents.

Check that you are not in breach of any covenant in force on your house, be it rented or bought, as to what you may or may not do there. Look at your lease or the deeds of the house. If the title to the house is registered, an office copy of the register entries can be obtained from the Land Registry by completing form A44, available from HMSO and law stationers shops. A specific restriction may have been imposed by agreement between neighbours or a general one by the land developer when a housing estate was being built or a landlord may have inserted one in the lease for a particular tenant or property. In some circumstances, a relaxation may be permitted. Someone at the citizens advice bureau or a solicitor may help you to understand any obscure wording on a document.

Make sure that your building society or other mortgagee has no objections to your plans. When you applied for your mortgage, you probably said that the house was solely for your family's use as a residence. Most building societies would not object provided that any restrictive covenants were complied with.

planning permission

If you want to add an extra room or convert a garage or put up an outbuilding, you may need to obtain planning permission from the local authority as well as meeting the requirements of the Building Regulations (in Scotland, getting building control consent). If you are in doubt, ask the building inspector or planning officer of your local authority to let you know what, if anything, is necessary in your case.

You may have to get planning permission to change the use of your premises, even if you own the house. For instance, strictly speaking, you need planning permission to use your garage to store goods, or if you want to undertake activities which are not incidental to the use of your house for domestic purposes—selling things from your house or using one room as a workroom, for instance. But small-scale business use may not amount to a change of use.

A fee of £66 is payable to the local authority for an application for permission to make a 'material change of use' of premises. (This fee is not refunded if the application is refused.)

Whether permission is required or granted depends on a number of factors, including the extent and type of the activity, its likely effect on your neighbours, and whether there will be a marked increase in traffic or people calling. The local authority has discretion to allow or not allow according to its own criteria; if your application is refused, you have the right of appeal.

If you go ahead without the necessary approval, you may be fined and made to cease the activities and remove any buildings which are unauthorised.

If you do need (and get) planning permission for the new use of your premises, the planning department informs the rating authority who may notify the valuation officer. He may come to inspect the premises about reassessing the rateable value (or at least the part you are now using for your business). The rates you pay in the £ will go up from the lower domestic tariff to the commercial tariff for that part. For commercial property, too, rates can be paid in instalments, spread over a maximum of 10 payments through the year.

insurance

If you set up business in your home, on however small a scale, you are technically speaking invalidating your normal householder's insurance policy. The insurers must be told if any part of the building is to be used for any other purposes than normal residence.

Most insurance policies involve signing a declaration which reads something on the lines of: 'I declare that . . .' and then there are a lot of statements, including one that says that the building is occupied '. . . solely by myself and my family and no business is carried on therein'. It is no good saying 'Well, I'm not actually the insured—my husband is, so of course this is different'. As far as the insurance company is concerned, it is not different. The householder's insurance applies jointly and severally and covers the deeds and misdeeds of the insured and family. So, if one of you, or even one of your children, is using the house for business, the whole of your policy is technically invalidated and the insurers would be entitled to refuse a claim on your policy, even if it arose from something domestic, nothing to do with the business activities.

You are supposed to notify the insurers if you, or a member of the family, change occupation. For some activities carried on at home, and in respect of some professions—for instance, teaching, translating, typing—insurers will be willing (with some exclusions and perhaps a little extra premium) to go on covering the premises as though they were a private dwelling. However, a number of people coming in and out of your house on business will affect your insurance cover for theft and for liability to other people. The liability section of a householder's policy excludes liability for injury or damage arising from or incidental to the insured's trade, profession or business.

What extra insurance cover you should take out depends on the type of work you do at home and the equipment you have for it.

fire and burglary

When arranging a new policy, the insurers will be concerned

about extra hazards regarding fire and burglary. It is quite likely that they will ask to survey the premises, and may then stipulate additional protection as far as burglary is concerned, such as window locks, secure locks on front and back doors, and in some circumstances a burglar alarm system.

Some business activities done in the home add nothing to the fire hazard. But if you are doing craftwork, such as lampshade making or woodwork, you may well have on the premises a larger quantity than normal of adhesives. In ordinary domestic quantities, these substances are fairly innocuous, but in larger quantities, used continuously in one room where the air could be quite heavy with their fumes, they become a genuine hazard: many modern adhesives can be easily ignited by a pilot light, a cigarette or an electric fire. (And these fumes may be toxic as well as flammable.) There is a fire hazard in many plastic foams such as some that are used for stuffings and fillings. Also, it can be dangerous to keep equipment on stairs or in passageways, impeding safe routes of escape.

You can ask your insurers for advice on fire or burglary protection. Their advice is free and they are not going to report you to the local authority if it transpires that you are in breach of some bye-law or regulation—but they may refuse to insure you unless you comply. Similarly, the advice of the fire prevention officer of the county fire brigade is available free and so is advice from the crime prevention officer of the local police.

One point to be borne in mind when your work is at home is that if your home is damaged or destroyed, for whatever reason, you are also out of work. Your householder's policy helps to meet the cost of alternative accommodation for yourself and family while your home is being repaired. But it is most unlikely that you will be able to carry on your own business from the hotel or boarding house. To cover the extra expense of carrying on your money-earning activity elsewhere, you could take out loss-of-profits insurance—but check whether the cost of the premium is proportionate to your potential loss of earnings.

liability to others
For some work, public liability insurance is an essential. In the course of your activities, if you were to cause injury to your customers or the public or damage to their property, an action might be brought against you for compensation. Public liability insurance would take care of compensation and costs awarded against you and also the costs involved in your defence. In practice, the insurers would take over the claim at the outset.

You may become involved in liability to your customers or others for injury or damage arising out of the sale or supply of defective or unsuitable goods. Separate insurance for product liability can be obtained. Where other people work in their home for you, you may need product liability cover in case someone employed , for instance, to pack goods for you, made a mistake in packing and rendered the goods in some way dangerous or lethal.

For some occupations, liability insurance can be quite difficult to obtain; you may have to consult an insurance broker. In a newly started business, the insurance company has only your word for it that you will be conscientious and careful.

You have to tell the insurers the nature of your work and what materials and equipment you are using. Your premium will be calculated according to the risks involved and the limit of indemnity (that is, the maximum amount the insurers will pay out on a claim). £500,000 is usually regarded as the least for adequate cover.

Other people's property entrusted to you, for repair perhaps, is not covered by your householder's insurance for damage you may do to it, nor for its unexplained loss. But you may be able to take out a special extension to your insurance for this.

You should get cover for any liabilities arising from dealing with children, such as teaching them music or giving them extra tuition at home. All you may need to do is advise your insurers and get an extension to your existing householder's policy for this.

If you employ another person in your home as part of a business you are running from your home—not as a housekeeper or similar domestic employment, which is in a different category—you have by law to have employer's liability insurance. And in case they do some damage to a client while working on your behalf, or by their negligence cause your client to have an accident, make certain that this will be covered by your public liability insurance.

lost in the post

If your work entails sending things by post, this can cause problems if anything goes missing or arrives damaged.

Compensation for the market value up to a maximum limit of £20 is payable by the Post Office if a letter or parcel is lost or damaged in the post due to the fault of the Royal Mail, its employees or agents. If you need to claim, it helps if you have obtained a certificate of posting at the time.

The Post Office also has a compensation fee system for parcels, paying out according to the fee paid: fee 35p for compensation up to £70, fee 45p for up to £130, fee 65p for up to £230, fee 80p for up to £360 compensation.

Anything sent by first class letter post can be registered. The compensation limits are £650 or £1350 or £1850, for which the registration fees are £1.20 and £1.35 and £1.50 respectively.

For a charge (from 45p to £1.35), you can insure registered post through the Post Office for consequential loss from £1000 up to £10,000.

The Post Office has a free leaflet *How to send things you value through the post*, giving details of all the postal compensation schemes available, and a separate leaflet on consequential loss insurance.

For sending documents, plans, drawings, books, it may be worth asking an insurance company about transit insurance, which covers replacing or reconstructing documents lost or damaged in transit. It may be difficult when you first go into business because the insurers will want to know approximately how many parcels and of what value you are going to send during a year. The premium, subject to a minimum, will be adjusted at each renewal. There is a limit on the amount paid per packet and per occurrence. The documents do not necessarily have to be sent via the post office; packets sent by rail or private carrier are also covered, provided the insurers are informed.

use of the car

Assuming that you are going to use your car or estate car in connection with your work, check in whose name the policy is. Anybody who is covered by the insurance—policyholder, named driver, or anyone driving with permission—may drive for social, domestic or pleasure purposes. A policy will also allow use by the policyholder in person in connection with a business.

If the policyholder does not use the car for business purposes himself, the business use extension can be transferred without extra charge to another driver, provided that driver has the necessary clean driving and insurance record. But if the policyholder is using the car for business purposes, however little, this clause is, as it were, fully taken up and for another person also to use the car for business, an extra premium must be paid. More and more insurance companies are, however, allowing business use by both a policyholder and his or her spouse without extra charge, provided the insurers are notified. This applies to husband/wife only, not to any two named drivers, be they brother and sister or friends: they still need to have a special endorsement and pay an extra charge for both to use the car for business.

An ordinary policy for a private car specifically excludes commercial travelling, so you must be careful that you are not doing innocently what insurers and the law would call commercial travelling. As far as the motor insurance aspect goes, the line between commercial travelling and ordinary selling and delivering is a fine one. If you are using your car for even a little bit of delivering or collecting orders, tell the insurers. Do not try to hide anything—if you are involved in an accident and are found to be carrying goods when you should not be, for instance, you will have been driving uninsured. Describe exactly what you are doing and the approximate volume of business done in that way. If this amounts to commercial travelling, you will have to pay a higher premium (but you and the family can use the car for social purposes under the same policy).

Check that you are insured for loss of goods you are carrying, in case the parked car or van is broken into while you are making a call.

If you want to use a trailer, you should have no problems about insuring it provided your driving licence is clean and your accident record is good and you have a suitable towing vehicle. The insurance for a trailer is more or less all-risks cover, depending on the desirability of the contents to thieves (nothing will keep a really determined thief out of a trailer). You may need to take out separate goods-in-transit insurance. Third party risks are covered by the motor policy of the towing vehicle while the two are attached to each other. It is sensible to insure a trailer where you insure the car, to make matters simpler if you should need to claim.

money

As your business begins to increase, so will the amount of money that you have to handle. Personal money in the house—husband's, wife's, children's—up to a set amount can be covered under your householder's policy. For business money, however, a separate cash policy is necessary. For this, you have to give an estimate of the amount of money you take to the bank in any one week, or of the annual turnover.

You cannot insure large amounts of cash in your home even if you want to: £200 is about the maximum amount of business money or personal money that insurers will cover. But you can have your maximum of business money and your maximum of personal money in the house at the same time and, if you were to lose the lot, you would get paid in full.

Where large amounts of cash are kept on your premises, the house will be considered a target risk for break-ins. Your insurers may send round a surveyor and will expect various precautions to be taken.

As soon as money comes in, bank it. You can arrange with your bank for night safe facilities after hours; there is no charge for this. When carrying any amounts of cash, avoid using the same route regularly.

personal insurance

The crucial question that insurers ask someone applying for any form of sickness insurance is 'What are your weekly earnings?'. When you start working for yourself, you are unlikely to have any idea of just how much you are going to earn. And without being able to answer this question, you are unlikely to get anything but cover for the minimum amounts.

Insurers may be reluctant about accepting you for any sickness insurance at all if you are starting to work freelance at home. Personal accident cover is less useful but easier to obtain. Even so, it has always been rather difficult in the case of people without a set income, such as housewives.

When you have become your family's breadwinner or joint breadwinner, or simply a more important person moneywise, it may be worth considering taking out a policy that will provide either a lump sum or an income for your dependants should you die. Traditionally, most life insurance is a policy on the husband's life to provide income for the widow on his death. But a husband may be rendered financially insecure by the death of his wife, and either can take out a policy on the other's life.

Insurance companies offer pension schemes specifically directed towards the self-employed, to provide a cash sum on 'retirement' and/or a regular pension. There is tax relief on the premiums. This is a complex subject, and it is worth getting reliable advice on the various alternatives before committing yourself. The Consumer Publication *Approaching retirement* includes a section on pensions and life insurance policies for the self-employed and their special tax relief.

national insurance

When you start being self-employed, you should notify your social security office.

Self-employed people are required to pay class 2 national insurance contributions. DHSS leaflet NI41, available from social security offices, gives national insurance guidance for the self-employed.

It is possible to apply for exception from liability to pay class 2 national insurance contributions if your gross annual earnings are, or are likely to be, below a certain amount (£2250 in 1988/89). Before you apply, check whether being exempt will affect entitlement to any benefits, such as a retirement pension, you may have accrued from previous contributions. A married woman or a widow who has an existing right to reduced liability does not need to apply for exception on the grounds of small income. She remains covered for limited benefits by her husband's contributions. Leaflet NI27A gives information about exception for people with small earnings from self-employment.

To pay class 2 contributions, either you get a card from the social security office on which to stick a stamp (bought at the post office) for each week, or you can arrange for direct debit of a bank or Girobank account. The 1988/89 class 2 contribution rate will be £4.05 a week.

Even when you pay class 2 contributions, you will not be entitled to claim unemployment benefit. To claim sickness benefit when self-employed, you need to produce some evidence of your normal earnings—your latest tax return will be useful for this.

Your work from home may be in addition to an existing employment in which class 1 national insurance contributions are paid. If it is likely that the total of class 1 and class 2 contributions will exceed the maximum contribution payable under the national insurance regulations, you can apply for deferment of class 2 contributions in respect of earnings from work done at home. This avoids unnecessary payments and refunds. An explanatory leaflet NP28 *More than one job?* can be obtained from local social security offices.

As well as weekly class 2 contributions, a self-employed person becomes liable to an additional type of tax in the form of what is called a class 4 'contribution'. This is a percentage on annual profits or gains (not turnover) between certain amounts. For 1987/88, the contribution was 6.3 per cent on profits between £4590 and £15,340 in the year. It is collected by the Inland Revenue with schedule D income tax and does not bring entitlement to any state benefits. Leaflet NP18, available from tax offices as well as social security offices, deals with class 4 contributions. There is also an Inland Revenue leaflet (IR24) on the computation of profits for class 4 liability. Since 6 April 1985, there is tax relief on 50 per cent of any class 4 contribution—this amount is deducted in the assessment of taxable income.

what to call yourself

There is no statutory requirement now to register the name of a business—you can start trading under the name you choose without formality. But certain business names require the written approval of the Secretary of State before they can be used. These names are set out in regulations (SI 1685/1981, amended by SI 1653/1982, available from HMSO, 70p and 35p each respectively). Words requiring consent are those which give the impression that the business is connected with Her Majesty's Government or a local authority, which imply national or international pre-eminence, or governmental patronage or sponsorship, or business pre-eminence or representative status, or which imply specific objects or functions. For certain other words or expressions, a request must first be made to the specified relevant body—for instance, the Home Office for use of 'Royale' or 'Windsor' or 'Duke' or 'Police'.

Under the Companies Act, any business, large or small, which is carried on under a name other than that of its owner must display particulars of its ownership on its business premises and on its business stationery. In addition, these particulars must be supplied in writing, on request, to any customers or suppliers. If you run a business using your own surname (with or without forenames or initials), you are not affected by this requirement. But you would be if you added another word to your name such as 'Lamond Antiques' rather than trading as 'A. M. Lamond'. And a married woman who is normally known by her married name but who carries on business in her maiden name has to comply.

A pamphlet *Notes for guidance on business names and business ownership* is available free from the Department of Trade and Industry's **Companies Registration Offices**: 55 City Road, London EC1Y 1BB (personal callers only); 102 George Street, Edinburgh EH2 3DJ (personal callers or by post); Companies House, Crown Way, Maindy, Cardiff CF4 3UZ (telephone 0222 388588).

registering a trade mark

In addition to having your own business name, you may want to have a distinctive sign to identify your products. To protect any symbol, design or word that you choose, you can register it as a trade mark at the Trade Marks Registry. This entitles you to the exclusive right to use the mark in relation to the goods for which it is registered. Before doing so, it would be wise to check at the registry that a similar mark has not already been registered: a search in person costs 90p for each quarter of an hour in the search room.

The registrar will advise (fee £9) on the distinctiveness of a proposed mark: some devices and words are not allowed. The fee for lodging an application is £60, with a further fee of £84 when the mark is registered. If you want to use a name mark separate from a symbol, it is advisable to make a separate application for each as well as one for the combination.

Before being registered, the mark will be advertised in the *Trade Marks Journal*, and time allowed for anyone to oppose it.

Registration is initially for a period of seven years and can be renewed at fourteen year intervals after that.

Since 1 October 1986, it has been possible to register a trade mark in the UK for providing a service for reward. A service mark is a distinctive symbol used as a means of identification and it confers a statutory monopoly on the registered owner. There are eight classes: if the services provided fall into more than one class, a separate application must be made for each.

Free booklets *Applying for a trade mark* and *Applying for the registration of a service mark*, and details of the procedure and all the fees, are available from the **Trade Marks Registry**, The Patent Office, State House, 66-71 High Holborn, London WC1R 4TP.

getting known

Start promoting yourself in a small way by advertising on newsagents' window boards and in the local paper(s). In most localities, there are advertising papers which are distributed free to every house. Your local 'freebie' will probably be happy to write about you, particularly if you place a small advertisement.

You should put together a press release and send it to all local newspapers, following it up with a telephone call, to ensure that they take an interest. In the press release, cover what you do in brief sentences, under a heading. Make sure you end with your name and telephone number, even though it may be on your headed paper—the newspaper may print the press release in its entirety so if you leave your contact number out, you may not get results.

If what you do is unusual (canary-boarding or sail-mending, say) send a note with details (and perhaps a photograph) to the features editor of the local newspaper, or to the local radio station. It is always worth contacting local papers: they have to have something to write about, and a new venture of almost any sort is news—locally, that is. Editorial mention is free publicity and can bring in a lot of business.

You can take a few lines in the personal or classified column or invest in a semi-display advertisement. Repeat at intervals if you want to keep your name before the public. If you take a standing advertisement (that is, one that is repeated every day or week, preferably on the same page of the paper), you will get a discount. It may be wiser not to book a very long run at one go, in case the first adverts generate too many enquiries for you to cope with.

A booklet *The small businessman's guide to advertising*, which presents the pros and cons of various forms of advertising and gives advice on the most efficient way to get your message across, is available free from Thomson Directories, 296 Farnborough Road, Farnborough, Hants GU14 7NU.

For some occupations, there are specialist magazines, and it may be worth investing in a few advertisements in an appropriate one or in one for an allied trade. Consult the classified index in the annual *Willing's Press Guide* in the public reference library, to find out what magazines, journals, newsletters and other publications there are. Current advertising rates are given in *British Rate and Data* (monthly), which also should be in the library.

Offer to visit local groups (mainly women's) to talk about what you do. Many groups are on the lookout for speakers for an evening or afternoon, to fill their calendar of events. Generally, they pay the speaker's expenses. Take examples of your work and a handout with your name and address.

You may be able to make a handbill advertisement yourself by using stick-on lettering or typing it and getting it photocopied.

Dressmaking, alterations and repairs
Wedding dresses a speciality

JANE A SMITH

20 High Street, Newtown
telephone Newtown 610

You could employ a schoolboy or girl to distribute your handbill to every possible interested person locally. For example, if you type, get the distributor to push one through every office door in the area; if you are a home hairdresser, get them put through the letter boxes of local residential homes. You have to assume you will get response so you must be prepared to handle a lot of work.

The Post Office operates a household delivery service which provides for the delivery of unaddressed advertising material on a door-to-door basis. The items do not have to be enveloped and they are delivered with the daily post to any size of area, from a postcode sector upwards; the minimum charge is £100. Alternatively, if you want to send out personally addressed items, you may be eligible for the Post Office's introductory offer for first-time users of direct mail. By making it easier and cheaper for people to respond to your advertisements, you can increase the number of enquiries you receive by using the Royal Mail's business-reply and 'freepost' services. Information about these services, and other postal services relevant to small businesses, is given in the Post Office's *Inland Compendium*, a free booklet available at any post office, and further details about any specific services can be obtained from the local postal sales representative.

It is a good idea to have business cards describing your services:

Peter Hardy
'The Knoll'
Oak Tree Lane
Little Wallington VZ3 5EE
telephone
Blasted Heath (023 862) 317

qualified translator—swedish, russian, german—
technical reports and business correspondence
work done promptly and typed efficiently

Have your business cards with you at all times. Do not put yourself in the position of not being able to promote yourself when an opportunity presents itself: even at parties, you may meet someone who needs your service. Give a card to satisfied customers to pass on.

putting up a sign

Before you put up a sign or other notice advertising your activities, check whether this comes within the advertising control system under the Town and Country Planning (Control of Advertisements) Regulations 1984, administered through local planning authorities - normally, the appropriate district council or London borough.

Some advertisements are exempt; for some, consent is 'deemed', provided it is within the rules; for all other types of display, express consent has to be applied for and a fee paid to the planning authority (for example, £18 for a business placard or direction sign, £66 for any other poster or board or sign).

A Department of the Environment booklet *Outdoor advertisements and signs: a guide for advertisers*, explaining the system of control and when consent is required and how to apply, is available from local planning authorities.

You could buy space outside other people's premises, such as newsagents and shops that can have boards standing outside. You would need to buy a board about 3ft × 1½ft and get the art work done. The response may be better than press advertising because the board is where people may pass it every day until the day comes when they need you.

selling your work

If what you will be offering is not a service but a product, you have to decide how to sell what you make. This may be by working to specific orders only, or going out to find a buyer when you have the goods ready.

You may get orders either direct by promoting yourself, or through some form of middleman (such as a shop, gallery, agent). Similarly, if you produce things on spec, you can sell them either via a middleman or direct. Be brave and confident of your product.

When you sell via a middleman, an individual agent or a shopkeeper sells what you have made, either buying outright from you or selling for you on commission, perhaps on a sale-or-return basis. But be aware of the risk of damage to the goods or their getting soiled.

An advantage of selling via an agent or middleman is that you do not need to use up time and energy in looking for individual outlets and will benefit from the agent's contacts and experience. However, you may not be allowed or able to set the price and the agent will take a commission. The workflow is out of your control and may be spasmodic and the agent may suddenly withdraw. If you are successful, you may be under pressure to produce in quantity, and to meet deadlines not of your own choosing.

When selling direct to the client, you are in charge of the whole operation and can do it in your own time and way. But it is time-consuming and you may get the pricing wrong until you are experienced. You may need a car or some other form of transport to get to, say, a local market.

If the customer comes to your home, you do not waste time and energy in travelling and can assess his needs individually. However, you may have to organise appointments, and visits may be time-consuming and interruptive. Not only do you have to have a suitable room, but also to keep the whole place – and yourself – reasonably tidy. Neighbours may not like the comings and goings, and you may find that you need planning permission for this use.

trades unions

With some activities, it may be difficult to place your work if you are not a member of the relevant trade union. Conversely, some unions do not accept someone for membership who is not already active in the particular trade. And a few unions do not accept people who are self-employed or freelance.

For instance, for illustrative or photographic work, the National Union of Journalists or the National Graphical Association would be the relevant unions; for writing, the National Union of Journalists or the Writers' Guild of Great Britain. To get machine knitting work at home, you may need to join the National Union of Hosiery and Knitwear Workers, and for dressmaking or repair work, the National Union of Tailors and Garment Workers. Overall, the General, Municipal etc Workers Union (GMB) is concerned about people who work at home, and other unions are increasingly involved with homeworkers.

Any union takes protective action on behalf of its members where there are difficulties over payment, conditions of work, contracts, statutory requirements, legal problems.

Information about the various unions, and head office addresses, are obtainable from the **Trades Union Congress** organisation and industrial relations department, Congress House, Great Russell Street, London WC1B 3LS. Most unions have branch offices for each area of the country, and you may be able to get in touch direct with the appropriate branch through your local telephone directory.

the telephone

The telephone is likely to become an essential factor in your activities. You may want to have an extension telephone in the room you are using for work. This will cost you (excluding VAT) £25 for the new plug-in socket; the cost of the actual instrument depends on the model you choose. When having a new extension socket fitted, your existing telephone will have to be converted to a plug-in type at the same charge, and additional sockets can be added at the same time for an installation charge of £25 each. If you still have the old style terminal blocks and sockets in your home, you cannot install new telephones or an answering machine until you have the new style sockets.

If you become established enough to justify the outlay, you can have a separate business line brought into the house, with a different number and listing in the telephone directory. A business line entitles you to an entry, free of charge, in the Yellow Pages directory under the classification of your choice as well as the normal entry in the alphabetical pages of the local telephone directory. In addition, you can pay for a semi-display advertisement in the Yellow Pages. The basic quarterly rental for a business line is £22.55 plus VAT; ask your area telephone sales office what the connection charge would be—it can be as much as £115, plus VAT.

There are also facilities on business lines for incoming calls to be transferred to another number either by the operator or, for calls on the same exchange, by a special switch system on the telephone. Information about subscriber controlled transfer of telephone calls can be obtained from the British Telecom area sales office.

There is a British Telecom leaflet showing all the telephones they have for sale and/or rent. Nowadays you can also buy telephones from independent suppliers. Make sure any telephone you buy is approved by the British Approvals Board of

Telecommunications and carries the BABT approval label with a green circle. There is a wide range of approved telephones, many of them with useful features such as memory for your most frequently used numbers and a last number re-dial facility. A cordless telephone which you can carry about with you to any room in the house and out into the garden could be useful. Other useful equipment for small business use are 'call loggers' which count and cost your calls, and if you are likely to have a lot of calls to make, a device that makes all your calls for you, letting you know when you are through and to which number: all you have to do is to key in the calls you want to make and it does the rest until you have got through to all your numbers.

A report in *Which?* in November 1987 assessed the different designs and facilities of the telephones on the market; one in February 1987 reported on cordless telephones.

The Telecommunications Industry Association (01-351 7115) can give information about items of equipment and the names of independent contractors.

using the telephone
Ensure that you have an up-to-date dialling code book (free from your telephone area office) and all the directories you are likely to need—some extra directories are free.

It is worth taking trouble to develop a good telephone manner. Be pleasant and friendly, but businesslike and firm at the same time. Try not to get involved in long-drawn-out conversations—this is a waste of your (by now valuable) time, and means that the line is blocked for other callers. Have a list or memorise the salient facts you need to know or to give an enquirer, be clear about your charges and conditions, about arrangements for collection or delivery, about timing and special requirements.

Keep a calendar or desk diary beside the telephone, and never fail to put down an order or appointment as soon as it is made. Train other members of your household, who may answer the telephone when you are out or busy, to do likewise and to be accurate and reliable over taking and giving messages. Make sure there is always a pad and pencil beside the telephone.

If you have to make telephone calls which are likely to be lengthy or are outside your local area, try to time them so that you take advantage of the cheaper rates: after 6 pm (cheapest) or between 8 and 9 in the morning or between 1 and 6 pm. The most expensive period is between 9 am and 1 pm.

answering machines

There are answering sets on which you can pre-record a message for callers in your absence and which record any messages from your callers. Try to record your own message and instructions to callers pleasantly so as not to put them off.

Answering machines can be bought from British Telecom: the sales office of your telephone area can supply a leaflet and information about the models available and charges. Many types of answering machines, with a versatile range of features, are available from independent commercial firms, to rent or to buy outright.

costing your work

One of the most difficult points for someone who has not previously worked on his or her own, or asked for payment for any product or service provided, is to know how much to charge. Even if you have previously done the same thing in the role of an employee (a typist or hairdresser, for example), it is not easy to assess what your work has really cost.

There are many elements to bear in mind. Look at your method of working, stage by stage, and check what you put into it in the way of actual materials (specially bought and from stock), incidentals, overheads, time; add an amount for clear profit.

Make enquiries from other people giving the same service.

time

To work out the financial loss or gain of an hour spent on a task, as well as the time spent in doing the actual work, you should cost in the time used for promoting yourself, getting the order for that particular job, any paperwork involved. Until you have done enough to realise how much you can make in an hour of your time, it is probably impossible to set an hourly rate for yourself.

If your customers do not come and collect from you, delivering the goods can prove quite expensive, in terms of your time as well as petrol or fares. It may not be acceptable to charge for this as a separate item, so you must incorporate an approximate amount for cost of delivery.

overheads

Another element difficult to disentangle will be your overheads: lighting and heating the room(s) you use, the higher rates you may be paying on that part of your premises, the telephone rental and, with machine work, the electricity consumed. You may also be using storage space—in garage or attic or cellar or garden shed—which would otherwise be utilised differently by you or your household, but this 'loss' is almost impossible to translate into financial terms. With some jobs, special cleaning of the workroom or equipment may be required, or maintenance of a machine, and this expense ought to be taken into account, too.

You may have to build an allowance for bad debts into your costing structure, and remember to allow for the fact that you may not be paid until some time after you send in a bill.

materials and equipment

If you are extending a hobby or spare-time interest, you are likely to have at least the basic necessary equipment, and experience in using it. You may have to buy more, larger, better, more versatile, more efficient versions, or extras.

The cost of the extra equipment you buy should be taken account of in your charges, and also its depreciation. To work out depreciation approximately, you should estimate how long you expect to be able to use the article and how much you may be able to get for it when you come to sell. Deduct the selling figure from the buying cost and divide the difference by the number of years of anticipated use. Supposing the price you pay is £150, you estimate using it for 5 years and that you will then be able to get £60 for it:

£150 − 60 = 90 ÷ 5 = £18 p.a. depreciation.

(If, however, there is no re-sale value at the end of your years' use, you would have to average out the full cost—in this case, £30 a year.)

Also, you should allow for loss on capital. If, instead of using the money for buying the equipment, you had invested the lump sum at, say, 7 per cent, you have to add the notional loss of interest in your costing: in this case, £10.50 p.a. Therefore, you should recover through your charges in each year £28.50 spread over each working day or working hour. (If you had to borrow money to buy the equipment, the interest charged is not a notional but an actual cost.)

As well as the amount of your time spent on paperwork, you should keep a note of the paper and envelopes you use for letters and accounts, the stamps, packaging materials, files and other office stationery (erasers, staplers, clips, glue, writing implements, batteries for calculator). In some cases, there may be a specific outlay on a particular job (telephone calls, for instance, or a series of letters), but in others you will have to assume a total figure and spread it out to add a fraction to your overall charge per job. This may be difficult to calculate until you know how many jobs you are going to get through in a month or year.

supplies

When the work involves making something, it should not be too difficult to work out how much you have spent on the materials or ingredients. If you have bought your supplies in bulk, you will have to break down the total outlay into smaller units for charging to each job. Even apparently minor items, such as thread, string, nails, adhesive, mount up into an accountable factor. With some work, you have to buy the materials some time before you are going to use them or be able to charge for them, and this capital loss should, strictly, be allowed for.

Where it is up to you to provide the raw materials, make use of any bulk or wholesale supplies available. You may qualify for trade discount and be able to buy at cash-and-carry stores.

A cash-and-carry store sells items at wholesale prices, in bulk, to bona fide traders (some also allow members of the public to buy direct). Find out whether there is one near you for the goods you need (look in the Yellow Pages directory) and telephone to ask what are the terms for traders. Some warehouses require evidence in support of your claim to be a trader, in the form of headed stationery or printed card, invoices with your business name, VAT registration number, bank or other references. You may be issued with a card to present whenever you go to buy, to prove your credentials as a trader.

Try to establish a good relationship with a reliable supplier (or two) so that you do not have to fail on a job because a supplier has let you down or there is an unaccountable delay in getting delivery of an essential material or ingredient (sugar or paper or upholstery tacks). Keep a close watch on your stocks and check regularly to see whether anything vital is running low.

If you are pricing something from materials you have in stock, allow for the price you will have to pay when you restock to carry out further orders.

dealing with customers

An essential principle is to meet all deadlines: if you allow yourself to fail to deliver on tne appointed date (or even hour), you will never make a success of your venture. Try to be firm when asked to do a rush job and do not take it on if it means falling behind with another job to which you are already committed. Ideally, you should establish a steady workflow, but this is unlikely to be possible in practice and there are bound to be emergencies and unforeseen delays or difficulties.

Whenever feasible, allow a 'fail safe' period in your timetable for each job, so that if there is a power cut, a machine break-down, a family crisis, you have time in hand to catch up. Remember that 'flu or a heavy cold in winter could throw you out of action for up to a week. Your timetable must include days off and a holiday (or two).

charging

You may find it difficult and embarrassing at first to look someone in the eye (particularly a friend) and say 'That will cost you £xx, please'. But the firmer and more clearcut you can be over the transaction, the less awkward it will be. It is no good being diffident or apologetic—this may even make the other person doubt your ability, and your price.

You may have to give an estimate before being given an order and then charge specifically after you have completed the job. Until you have had some experience of the costs involved, try not to estimate too precisely because it will be difficult to be accurate enough to be fair to yourself or to your customer. Give an approximate range of the likely cost, making it clear that the final figure may vary upwards or downwards. Once a firm quotation is accepted, you are bound by it.

Compare what professionals in the same line of business are charging with what you would have to charge for such work to make your venture profitable. You can then uprate or downrate yourself according to the circumstances. This applies especially to a service or skill that does not end up in a visible product: for example, being a consultant or an agent, a teacher or researcher, a repairer or hirer, a minder or landlady. As a general rule, people employing your services will have a fair idea of the going rate, and that may determine what you can charge. If they do not want to pay the reasonable price that you have so carefully decided upon, then let them go elsewhere. You will gain respect, not lose it, by being firm and unembarrassed about pricing your work.

Do not knowingly undercharge, even to begin with when you may be feeling unconfident about your abilities. It may create ill feeling and loss of custom if you then suddenly increase your charges sharply for the next or subsequent orders.

It is generally better to stick to the charge or scale you have decided to adopt, regardless of who the customer is. It will bring accounting complications if you vary according to the recipient for each job, and may well arouse ill will and lead eventually to loss of custom.

asking for payment

If you have established a scale of charges—for example, for photographic work, bed and breakfast, hairdressing, kennelling —have it printed or typed for customers to look at.

Where your costs vary according to the season (in cooking perhaps because the ingredients are seasonal), you have to decide whether to vary your prices, too, or spread the higher costs over the whole year.

It is likely that it will be up to you to introduce the subject of payment. Do so as early as is tactful in the proceedings, so that there is no misunderstanding or waste of time over whether the customer can afford what you are offering. Make sure that people know what your charges are when they telephone, even if they do not ask. It is generally a good idea to confirm in writing.

Specify clearly what you are charging for, including materials where appropriate. There may be items which your customer will see as 'hidden extras' but which you consider obvious expenses: pills for the cat you are boarding, for instance, or tacks and braid for an upholstery job, or the ream of paper for typing a thesis. If the stationery or whatever you need is not provided, buy it and get a receipt to attach to the bill so that the client can see exactly what he is paying for over and above the actual work.

When the time comes for payment, be businesslike about presenting your bill: preferably, have it written out (or typed) and ready for your customer when the work is delivered or collected. Keep a copy. Unless you have headed stationery, make sure that your name and address appear on the bill; also, your telephone number (for repeat orders).

Bills that you send to the customer, rather than hand over for immediate payment, should state clearly that you require payment within, say, three weeks. Offering a discount for prompt payment may be an incentive, but you must allow for this in your costing.

Always keep a record of what you have been paid, for what, by whom and how, particularly if it is a cash transaction. It may be tempting just to pocket the notes without showing their receipt in your accounts, but you will end up with tax queries as well as accountancy problems if you do this.

It is unlikely that anyone paying you personally for work you have done in your home will try to pass off a dud cheque on you, but have no compunction about asking to see a cheque card. Compare the signatures and write the card number yourself on the back of the cheque in case you need to invoke the bank's guarantee. If you are in any doubt about a customer's financial integrity or standing, or if he or she is a total stranger to you, do not accept a cheque for any amount over the £50 limit guaranteed by the card: insist on cash instead. Even if a cheque turns out to be dud, however, it should not be thrown away because it is evidence of an agreed debt.

Where the job is a long-drawn-out one or is being done in stages, you should arrange for part-payment, in advance or at an intermediate stage, otherwise you will be out of pocket for too long. You may run into 'cash flow' problems (that is, lack of ready money available), especially if you have had to pay out for materials or another person's work long before you get paid yourself. You may need to ask for an advance of cash in order to buy materials that you do not have in stock. Some firms settle their invoices only once a quarter; if you get an order from a large firm, ask about their timing of payments.

It is important to keep a steady eye on your outgoings and incomings, to make sure that there is a reasonable balance between the two and that you are not subsidising your customers by mistake. The real state of your financial affairs will not emerge for some months, or even years, but you should check the position regularly—monthly, or even weekly.

bad payers

There will inevitably be a number of bad debts which have to be written off. Do not send more than one stamped reminder—if subsequent ones go unstamped, there is hope that the debtor will take notice.

You can try to get your money by telephoning—but you may have to telephone and telephone and telephone. Tell anyone who answers the telephone why you are 'phoning, even though you may feel awkward when you have to speak to someone who is not responsible for the non-payment: you may embarrass your non-payer into paying, by telling members of the household that he or she owes you money.

If you are willing to spend a few pounds on a county court summons, or a solicitor's letter, this may lead to sudden payment by the debtor. Do not hesitate to sue if your client still does not pay. You are not risking much by losing a client who does not pay.

Keep a black list, and refuse to do further work for a debtor, at least not until the previous account is settled or unless payment is made in advance. Where possible, alert others who may have dealings with the person. If the work came via an advertisement, notify the publication concerned: they may be able to apply pressure on your behalf or at least warn others.

The *Which? Tax-Saving Guide*, published each March, explains how bad debts can, in certain circumstances, be claimed as a business expense for tax purposes.

KEEPING ACCOUNTS

You should keep a careful record of all financial transactions concerned with your work. This is important not only to check whether you are making a profit or loss but also because of legal requirements either now or later.

As soon as you start to earn or pay out any money at all, keep a record of all expenses and payments as they arise. Make sure that the full date is on everything. Fill in cheque stubs and paying-in slips clearly and fully.

A simple ruled cash book may be enough to start with: you can enter what you have earned at one side and at the other enter expenses, with dates and any other relevant details. Keep distinct records of cash and banking transactions. All money received (cash and cheques) should be paid in, even if you then withdraw it again.

What records need to be kept will be dictated by the volume of work involved. For instance, a writer whose year's work produces, say, one book may have just a single receipt of cash from the publisher with few expenses—perhaps paper, typewriter ribbons, postage, fares. On the other hand, someone doing hairdressing will have lots of regular small receipts of cash and numerous payments for stock, equipment, telephone, and would need a more elaborate cash book for payments, VAT records, and so on.

It is wise to write up your account books at least once a week. Where applicable, the following should be recorded, with dates:

- payments made for stock
- payments made for other purchases or services
- money received and from whom
- goods or services supplied and to whom
- cash drawn for personal use.

Although records can be simple, they must be comprehensive and capable of providing information for income tax purposes and for value added tax (or, if VAT registration is not yet required, capable of being adapted later to provide the necessary information).

If you decide that more elaborate records are necessary, go to a stationer's or office equipment shop and examine what cash record books and account books are available. A loose-leaf analysis book with, say, 4 columns for receipts and 16 columns for payments enables you to keep a cumulative check on how your venture is proceeding (with a cross-check for arithmetical accuracy) and also provides the figures you may need for submission to bank manager, accountant, Inland Revenue, Customs and Excise (for VAT).

You must keep all invoices, bills, copies of receipts given, cheque stubs, letters, and anything else at all relating to your takings and expenditure. File them in date order. If not many, they can be put into a folder or box file or on a spike; or keep them in a ring binder, numbered and cross-referenced to your account books.

It is a good idea to separate the papers for each accounting year so that when you come to make your declaration of income for tax purposes, you will have all the relevant material to hand and will not have to go ferreting amongst all your bills and letters to find out how much you earned in a preceding year. Keep everything for at least six years. The Inland Revenue (and Customs and Excise for VAT) have the right to examine your records at any time and you are obliged to produce relevant information on demand.

Always make a note of any item that might possibly be allowable for tax purposes. It is difficult to get a claim allowed for any items if they have not been recorded in the business books.

Be especially careful to record all expenses that relate to your work where part of your business expenses come out of the household account, such as electricity or telephone bills. You will need some record of all such expenses when compiling a claim for tax allowances.

The money that comes in and goes out for your work should be kept strictly separate from your personal and household finances.

Have two cheque books and paying-in books, using one for business and one for private payments.

Or you could open a separate bank or Girobank account for your business finances, or an instant-access building society account. (Some banks charge for each transaction until or unless you keep in your current account more than the bank's minimum for charging.) Check at regular intervals that the balance in the business account agrees with your account books.

It is sensible to set aside in a savings deposit account some money to meet tax and VAT liabilities as and when these fall due.

having an accountant
It could be worthwhile to get a qualified accountant to advise and help you on the best method of keeping proper accounts and how to claim any expenses allowable against tax for the self-employed.

If you know an accountant or book-keeper who is working at or from home, ask for his or her help with your accounts—and pay the appropriate fee for this professional service. A book-keeper can show you how to keep your accounts, an accountant may be able to help also with advice on some other aspects of your financial affairs.

Personal recommendation is generally the safest way of finding an accountant. If you do not know of one, the bank manager or solicitor may be able to suggest someone. But try to find out whether the particular accountant you have been told about is experienced in the kind of accounting or tax work your venture entails.

Accountants may now advertise their services in a limited way in the local press and in the Yellow Pages telephone directory. Or you can write to the **Institute of Chartered Accountants** (in England and Wales: PO BOX 433, Moorgate Place, London EC2P 2BJ; Scotland: 27 Queen Street, Edinburgh EH2 1LA) or to the **Chartered Association of Certified Accountants** (29 Lincoln's Inn Fields, London WC2A 3EE) and ask for the address of the nearest district society to get the names of qualified accountants in your area.

When first contacting a firm of accountants, make it clear that you need somebody who knows about the financial aspects of a self-employed or freelance person. An accountant knowledge-able about the hazards and complexities of self-employment can save you a lot of money as well as time; one who specialises in a different area could be unaware of all the pitfalls and possibilities.

Professional accountants charge on an hourly basis, according to seniority and type of work, plus expenses. There is no fixed scale, but allow for at least £20 an hour, plus VAT. Specify (preferably in writing) what work you want an accountant to do for you and ask what his charge is likely to be. His bill should be itemised according to the work you have agreed between you — for example, giving advice, preparing tax return, dealing with value added tax, any other book-keeping matters.

the accounting year
With the possible exception of the first year, your accounts should run for a 12-month period which begins and ends on the same date each year. But your accounting year need not necessarily be the calendar year 1 January to 31 December nor need it coincide with the tax year (6 April to 5 April).

Because of the way in which self-employed tax assessments are made, substantial tax advantages or disadvantages can result from the selection of the annual accounting date, particularly if the business is seasonal. Generally speaking, choose a date for the beginning of the first accounting period that gives greater emphasis to low rather than high earning periods. For example, for a high period during the summer months, it would probably be better to choose the end of May as the annual accounting date; if the business started in January, the first accounts would then cover a period of 17 months; if the business started in September, the first accounts would cover the 9-month period to the end of May. But if the business started in May, it would normally be unwise to select a date beyond the following May because this would result in two high periods being included in the calculations as the basis for the first three years' tax assessments.

tax

The *Which? Tax-Saving Guide*, published in March each year, includes tax if you are self-employed or do any freelance work.

The Inland Revenue has a free pamphlet *Starting in business* (IR28 available at tax offices and at Somerset House, London WC2R 1LB), which gives an outline of how tax is assessed on profits, what records should be kept, allowable expenses, payment of tax, and includes advice about VAT and national insurance. In it there is a copy of form 41G which you should use to notify your local inspector of taxes (listed in the telephone directory under Inland Revenue) as soon as you start to work on your own. There is also leaflet IR57 *Thinking of working for yourself?* which is an abridged and simplified version of IR28.

Annual accounts will have to be submitted to the tax inspector, giving details of your trading profit. The accounts need not necessarily be professionally prepared but they must be clearly set out and accurate. (The local tax office can be asked for advice about preparing accounts for your tax return.) If you decide to use an accountant, he will not only do the accounts but also will negotiate with the taxman on your behalf. But even if he does all the work for you, it is you who will remain responsible to the Inland Revenue.

If you are genuinely self-employed, you will be taxed under schedule D. This may allow you to claim tax relief on more expenses than if you were an employee and taxed by PAYE under schedule E.

To be considered self-employed, you have to prove to the taxman's satisfaction that no one person has sole rights to your working time. Therefore, try to get work from several sources and pay your own national insurance stamp.

Whether you are employed or self-employed depends on the terms of the particular engagement entered into. If you supply a service to only one, or predominantly to one customer, a formal letter or contract might clarify your position as an independent, self-employed contractor.

The Revenue's leaflet IR56 *Tax: Employed or self-employed?* gives some guidance on how to decide. It includes questions to ask yourself to check whether you are likely to count as self-employed, such as

o are you ultimately responsible for how the business is run?
o do you risk your own capital in the business?
o are you responsible for bearing losses as well as taking profits?
o do you yourself control what you do, whether you do it, how you do it, and when and where you do it?
o do you provide the major items of equipment needed for the job? (not just the small tools which many employees provide for themselves)

If you are in any doubt about your self-employed status from the tax point of view, get in touch with your local tax office for advice.

tax in the first years
If you do isolated freelance or spare-time work, you will be taxed on the profit you make in the current tax year (6 April to 5 April). If you are also an employed person, the tax on your spare-time profits may be collected through the PAYE system.

If your self-employed activities are a proper business, adding up to more than occasional freelance work, you will normally be taxed on what is called a preceding year basis: a tax bill for the 1987/88 tax year, for example, will be based on the profit made in the accounting year which ended during the 1986/87 tax year. For the first years of the business, there are special rules for assessing the tax due, based on the first or immediately preceding 12 months, depending on when the end of your accounting period falls (leaflet IR28 gives details, with examples).

Since the profits of the first 12 months in business are used in calculating three years' assessments, it is best to keep them as low as possible. With some activities, the profits vary according to the time of year: the best earning period may be just before Christmas, or more work might be done in the summer than in the winter. If your accounting year starts just before the 'best time' (which in the first year is not likely to be very profitable anyway), the second 'best time' is not included in the first year's trading.

If you intend to use an accountant, it would be wise to consult one at this early stage, since the starting date and the date of the first accounts can be significant, and there are various tunes that can be played using the opening bases of assessment.

There are also special rules for the tax years immediately preceding the date when a business ceases.

wife's earnings

Even where a wife is earning money for herself by working freelance or running a business on her own, it is her husband who normally has to pay the tax due on her profits. He can claim wife's earned income allowance on her earnings as well as claiming the married man's personal allowance. (Although the earned income allowance is claimed by the husband, it is set against the wife's earnings.)

A husband and wife can choose to have the wife's earned income taxed separately, instead of the wife's earnings being aggregated with her husband's income for tax. But this is an advantage only for a couple who are in a high-rate tax category. The application to be taxed separately has to be made jointly, not earlier than six months before or not later than twelve months after the relevant tax year; the wife's earnings will continue to be taxed separately until a joint notice of withdrawal is given. Leaflet IR13 deals with *Wife's earnings election*.

allowable business expenses

Certain expenses you incur in the course of your work can be deducted from your takings to arrive at the amount of your income liable for tax.

The sort of expenses you can claim for are the materials needed for your work, heating and lighting the room you work in, the telephone, travel in connection with your work, clothes specially required for the work, specialist books or magazines, and the premiums for insurance relating wholly to your business.

However, when you have been using part of your home exclusively for business (claiming tax relief on rates and rent for this), should you later sell the home, you do not get exemption from capital gains tax on that part of it. If, for instance, you had a five-roomed house and used one room of it exclusively for your work, one-fifth of any profit on selling the home would be subject to CGT. A leaflet (CGT8) on capital gains tax is available free from tax offices.

Although the rules for deducting an item as a business expense are that it is 'wholly and exclusively for the purposes of the trade', you can, in many cases, obtain the Inland Revenue's agreement to a claim for a proportion of expenditure for something you use partly for business and partly for private purposes. This is quite specifically a concession and not an entitlement as of right—but claim, and be prepared to have it disallowed. It is better for a claim to be disallowed by the tax inspector than not to try—you will not be told by the Inland Revenue if you have omitted to claim for a permissible item.

If you will be claiming part of the cost of your car as a business expense, keep a mileage record distinguishing between business and personal use so that you can extricate the business percentage for your tax claim.

The cost of buying equipment or machinery for the purposes of the business—a typewriter, sewing machine, calculator, photocopier, kiln—is not an allowable business expense, but qualifies for a writing-down allowance of 25 per cent, from the accounting year in which the item is bought.

The table on pages 54 and 55, based on the *Which? Tax-Saving Guide*, summarises what is normally allowed and not allowed by the Inland Revenue as a business expense.

personal pension
A self-employed person who is paying into an 'approved' personal pension or retirement annuity scheme can claim relief at his top rate of tax for the premiums being paid, provided these are under $17\frac{1}{2}$ per cent of net relevant earnings (a higher percentage for an older person; for example, someone born between 1916 and 1933 can pay in premiums up to 20 per cent of net relevant earnings). Tax relief not taken up in one year can be carried forward for up to six years.

the tax you pay

The law requires a taxpayer to notify the Inland Revenue of any new source of income within 12 months of the end of the tax year in which the income first arose, even if the inspector of taxes has not sent a tax return for completion, and irrespective of whether there is a profit or loss, and even if you do not yet have all the figures. The onus of notifying is specifically on the taxpayer and failure to do so can lead to penalties and payment of interest on arrears.

Your profit counts as your earned income and you are liable for tax on it in the same way as an employed person is on his salary and you pay at the same rates as anyone else, with the same personal tax allowances. (If you invest any of your profits, the interest counts as your investment income and you will be taxed accordingly.) Your taxable profit is the amount of money you have been paid for your work or services or are due to be paid on invoices you have already issued, less allowable business expenses.

Where your accounting year does not coincide with the tax year, it is the figures for the accounting year that you should supply to the Inland Revenue.

Do not risk underdeclaring your income. Even if you are sure that you have no tax liability because your takings have been so small, you must include the source of income on the tax return.

You will be required to pay tax in two instalments on or before 1 January (or 30 days after issue of the assessment, if that is later) and the following 1 July respectively. If you do not pay by the specified time, and have not appealed within 30 days and applied to postpone payment of some or all of the tax, the Inland Revenue may charge you interest on what you owe from those dates. There is an Inland Revenue form on which to make the appeal and apply for postponement. If your application for postponement is accepted, you are then only liable to pay the balance for which postponement has not been sought. If no application for postponement is submitted—whether the tax is excessive or not—you are legally obliged to pay the amount estimated by the inspector.

Inland Revenue investigations leaflets IR72 and IR73 deal respectively with 'The examination of business accounts' and 'How settlements are negotiated'.

If your venture turns out to have been running at a loss, you can ask for the loss to be set against any other taxable income for the year in which you made the loss. Such a loss will only be allowed if the inspector is satisfied that the business is being properly carried on on a commercial basis with a view to making a profit. Normally, the amount of the loss will be set against any profits in the following or subsequent years. A loss made in any of the first four years of assessment of a new business which might reasonably be expected to make a profit, can be set against other income you had in the three tax years before the year in which you made the loss. This will bring you a tax repayment from the Inland Revenue—but the calculations for such a tax rebate are complicated so you should ask the tax inspector for details, and consult an accountant.

loans

An advantage of having a bank account is that you may be allowed to operate with an overdraft should you have to pay out more than you get in for a while. But talk to the bank manager first. If you establish a good relationship with your bank manager and get him interested in your project, he may be a useful source of advice and information on your financial position and potential. You may be able to get a bank loan for a specific purchase or activity, such as an extension or adaptation of your premises.

You can claim as an allowable expense against tax any interest you pay on a loan or overdraft that is obtained solely for the business—for buying machinery or equipment, for example. The money must have been borrowed within a reasonable time of the purchase (generally, about three months).

When you approach someone for a loan, prepare a realistic report of your activities and plans, and the benefit you anticipate from the expenditure in question. Particularly when you are dealing with an intermediary, such as a bank manager, you will need to impress him with your abilities and potential because he is responsible to his superiors for lending you their money. You may be expected to provide reasonable security for the loan, such as your home or other property. Be careful to establish whether the rate of interest is fixed or variable, and note the annual percentage rate of interest (APR) that you will be paying, so that you do not find you are committed to higher repayment costs than you thought.

It is advisable to avoid spending more than is essential on capital expenditure when you start out on your venture. Excessive initial costs will tie up your money and you may find yourself working hard just to pay off a debt.

business expenses

	NORMALLY ALLOWED	NOT ALLOWED
Basic costs and general running expenses	Cost of goods bought for resale and raw materials used in business. Advertising. Delivery charges. Heating. Lighting. Cleaning. Rates. Telephone. Replacement of small tools and special clothing. Postage. Stationery. Subscriptions to professional and trade organisations. Relevant books and magazines. Accountant's fees. Bank charges on business accounts.	Initial cost of machinery, vehicles, equipment, permanent advertising signs. Cost of buildings.
Use of home for work	Proportion of telephone, lighting, heating, cleaning and insurance. Proportion of rent and rates, if use part of home *exclusively* for business—but claiming ground rent or rates may mean some capital gains tax to pay if you sell your home.	
Wages and salaries	Payments to employees or outworkers.	Your own wages or salary, or that of any partner.
Tax and national insurance	Employer's national insurance contributions for employees; 50% of class 4 'contributions'. VAT on allowable business expenses if not a registered trader for VAT.	Income tax. Capital gains tax. Inheritance tax. Your class 2 national insurance contributions.
Entertaining	Reasonable entertainment of overseas trade customers and their overseas agents (and normally your own costs on such an occasion).	Any other business entertaining—eg entertainment of UK customers.

	NORMALLY ALLOWED	NOT ALLOWED
Gifts	Gifts which advertise your business (or things it sells), costing up to £10 a year to each person. Gifts (whatever their value) to employees.	Food, drink, tobacco, or vouchers for goods given to anyone other than employees.
Travelling	Hotel, meals, travel expenses on business trips. Travel between different places of work. Running costs of own car: whole of cost if used wholly for business, proportion if used privately as well.	Cost of buying a car or van.
Interest payments	Cost of arranging and interest on overdrafts and loans for business purposes.	Interest on capital paid or credited to partners. Interest on overdue tax.
Hiring	Reasonable charge for hire of capital goods, including car.	
Insurance	Business insurance—eg employer's liability, fire and theft, motor, for employees.	Your own life, sickness, accident insurance.
Trade marks, designs and patents	Fees paid to register trade mark or design or to obtain patent.	Cost of buying patent from someone else.
Legal costs	Costs of recovering debts; defending business rights; preparing service agreements; appealing against rates on business premises.	Expenses of acquiring land, buildings or leases. Penalties for breaking the law. Costs of fighting tax case.
Repairs	Normal repairs and maintenance to premises or equipment.	Cost of additions, alterations or improvements.

CHOICE OF WORK

This book does not deal with the professions in which people are self-employed and work from home, using part of their home as surgery, studio, consulting room, drawing office. Some people have no choice: the nature of their gift entails working independently—artists, composers, creative writers, for instance. Most of the other professionals decide at the outset of their career whether to practise privately or with others. Only someone with professional qualifications, experience and contacts can take up such work, or return to it, on a freelance basis. The relevant professional body can provide advice and information for members who are thinking of setting up on their own.

with previous job experience

It may be possible to do at home the work in which you have been trained and previously employed. Generally, it would not be worth learning the job from scratch in order to make use of it at home, and certainly not to do it at home without previous experience.

beauty therapist, hairdresser

If you have been previously employed in any of the beauty professions—beauty therapist, beautician, electrolysist, manicurist, hairdresser—you may well be able to set yourself up for clients to come to you at your home.

You may need to have planning permission from the local authority for this use of part of your house or flat. Some local authorities also have bye-laws relating to hairdressing establishments and most require registration for ear-piercing and electrical epilation (electrolysis).

You should set aside a room as a treatment room, and have a room in which clients can wait. Where possible, choose rooms which can be approached without having to go through the rest of the house. There should be access to a lavatory with a washbasin.

The treatment room must have enough space for the washbasin and equipment you use in the course of the treatment, and storage space for supplies of preparations you use.

You must be on the telephone. Keep an appointment book beside the instrument.

Initial outlay will be on equipment from specialist suppliers, and on furniture, including mirrors and suitable chairs, and on the installation of basins with a constant supply of hot water, and electric sockets. Ongoing costs include the electricity for lighting and heating water and rooms and for driers and other apparatus. There will be laundry or washing costs for towels, wraps, linen. Supplies of hair preparations and cosmetics should be obtainable at wholesale prices.

Concentrate on local advertising, such as in newsagents' windows. A printed card with your name, address, telephone number and charges will augment word of mouth recommendations. Your charges should reflect those asked in the local salons.

insurance

You must notify your household insurers and be prepared to pay an additional premium for the extra risks, such as fire and damage to your equipment; cover for theft will be restricted.

Insurance is desirable for your liability to clients arising from negligence in a treatment given by you. This will be difficult to obtain unless you are qualified (and even if you are, some risks are excluded). A special policy can be obtained from Lloyd's through the Hairdressers Insurance Bureau (9–17 Perrymount Road, Haywards Heath, Sussex RH16 1TA) and a number of insurance companies offer special hairdressers' policies covering liabilities and the other risks you may need to insure for. A premium of £30 to £35 is likely to be charged for liability insurance if you are a qualified hairdresser, £50 to £55 if you are a qualified beauty therapist, to cover your liability for up to £250,000 in respect of the treatment risk.

The International Federation of Health and Beauty Therapists arranges a professional indemnity policy at Lloyd's, with a preferential rate for IFHB members.

You will probably also require general public liability insurance in case of an accident occurring due to a defect in your home, because a normal household policy will specifically exclude liability in connection with any business undertaken. An additional premium of around £8 would be charged for the public liability risk.

further training

For brushing up your skills, there are special short courses at colleges, local or in London, and courses for the City and Guilds certificates in beauty therapy, cosmetic make-up, electrical epilation, hairdressing, manicure.

The **International Health and Beauty Council** issues diplomas and certificates of competence to students who have passed their examinations in, for example, beauty therapy, facial treatment, make-up, manicure, epilation. The IHBC can let you have a leaflet *So you want to be a beauty therapist?*, with information on what the work and training involves, and also a list of courses at colleges in the UK recognised by the IHBC; send a 20p stamp to the IHBC, 109 Felpham Road, Felpham, West Sussex PO22 7PW. The **International Federation of Health and Beauty Therapists**, also at Felpham, in conjunction with the IHBC, is sponsoring the development of 'open learning' courses for refresher and updating training of beauty therapists. The **British Association of Beauty Therapy and Cosmetology** also can give information about courses (from the secretary, Suite 5, Wolseley House, Oriel Road, Cheltenham, Glos. GL50 1TH).

book-keeper

With experience in book-keeping, you can offer to help another freelancer or a small business with book-keeping problems, or do outwork for larger firms. The outlay is minimal—large desk or table, paper, pens, binders or files. Charge by the hour, and for expenses incurred for a particular job, such as telephone calls or fares, and for postage costs.

Advertise your services locally and in professional publications. You will need to keep your knowledge of tax requirements up-to-date.

If you are the owner of a computer, make sure you have a good book-keeping program. You can then offer

o to carry out home book-keeping services for local firms
o to run off monthly accounts, statistics, cash flow forecasts
o to set up systems for firms who are about to computerise.

computer work

You must know quite a bit about what you are doing before considering computer work at home. Do not get excited about the futuristic world of computers and glittering opportunities for yourself or your family: it is unlikely that you can embark on a computer career starting at home from scratch.

If you do have prior experience, you may be able to switch to home-based work. Even a small (in size and price) computer can accomplish tasks which a few years ago were the purview of large sophisticated specialist companies. But you will be competing with the computer manufacturers' hard sell of their package. So, think through your options carefully and practically so that you do not get caught by rapid obsolescence, small margins and the risk of being left with a product and service overtaken in the market place.

Your approach to earning money should be based on the need for your particular skill. You can probably master a different computer relatively easily, and the sort of action you need to take in getting started is

○ finding who wants your skill or service
○ getting enough clients or work to yield the earnings
○ choosing the right tool and paying for your equipment
○ getting set up and trained.

There are City and Guilds certificate courses in information technology, including computer programming and the use of micro-computers. Do not get caught by the blandishments of commercial training schools which can be very expensive and heartbreakingly disappointing. Go to your local technical college or ask the Manpower Services Commission, to find out about reputable (and cheaper) ways of getting training.

where to find work
Talk to people who already offer similar services. They may help without your needing to hide from them that you are interested in competing—and may even ask you to help them. Doing work at home on occasions can help to keep your hand in (even if earnings are less than you want) and will keep you 'on the books' for those times when you can get and do more.

You can try a direct approach to firms who may require your services, local enterprise agencies, chamber of commerce, bank managers, accountants. You may have to persevere until you find a firm willing to let you apply your skills from home. On the other hand, you may be welcomed with open arms, especially if you show willingness to fit in with their schedules.

The disadvantage of 'outwork' employment is usually that you are an overload resource and this means being dependent on the employer for amounts of work (and thus earnings) and also, if you are to succeed, being available when demand is there.

The **Association of Independent Computer Specialists** represents individuals and small firms, and is geared also to help the serious practitioner working independently at home. You can ask AICS Services (Leicester House, Leicester Street, London WC1H 7BN) to put you in touch with local members who can be a source of help and advice.

Many computer manufacturers promote user clubs for enthusiasts and these can be a useful contact point for turning a hobby activity into (smallish) profits.

what kind of work

Computer work done at home can cover all sorts of activity from the home computer hobbyist to the seriously employed computer specialist.

Obvious examples for using a home computer or a terminal for some professional or work function which you are qualified to do or can get trained for are typing and/or word processing; also book-keeping and accounting and financial 'spread sheet' services. You can go right up to offering to run packages on a small computer for anything from mail services to shops' stock control and invoicing.

Freelance independent specialist computer services that can be performed at home if you have previous experience include software development, programming, and a wide range of technical consulting services. The key issue is likely to be the proportion of time you are prepared and able to spend away from home 'on site'. It is essential to organise work so that your clients are satisfied with the extent to which you visit them to liaise on the services you perform.

Freelance contracting is now well established in the computer industry and there are specialist firms for part-time freelancers (for example, F International), although increasingly the logistics of specialist team work can make completely home-based work difficult. Members of a group such as AICS can help each other by work sharing; by careful planning so that parts of a job can be done off site; by using a team leader as representative on site.

A firm wanting to benefit from your skills should be organised to use you; it should also provide the means and not expect you to fork out for expensive equipment you need to use for their work. The logistics of doing computer-related work are relatively straightforward in these days of easy communications. There are special ways of linking a computer or terminal from home to a computer somewhere else. The simplest is an easy dial-up connection via your home, where the cost is borne by whoever dials—if you are lucky, they dial you.

You will need contact with your clients for getting and returning work: this requires flexibility, a willingness to fit in with those you are doing the work for, an organising approach and, usually but not necessarily always, your own transport. Some clients may do the fetching and carrying or be flexible enough to help you out by doing so on occasions.

linguist

With a good knowledge of a foreign language, you can either teach or take conversation classes, or set up as a translator.

Most translation work is technical. However good your command of the language, you also need specialist knowledge of particular subjects—about medicine or music, say. The most technical translations are the most highly paid (and the most difficult); some less usual languages such as arabic and japanese command higher rates. Professional translators normally only translate into their mother tongue rather than into the foreign language.

Stick to subjects you know, and do not take on things you are unfamiliar with 'just to oblige'—you are more likely to lose a disillusioned client than to oblige him.

If you are going to translate regularly, it is best to get yourself some professional qualifications, which will give you the recognition that you need. The Institute of Linguists provides professional examinations for general and technical translators as a qualification for membership of the Institute.

Some public libraries keep lists of people prepared to do certain jobs—the names of translators and interpreters, for instance. It costs nothing to have your name on the list.

There are a number of translation agencies who are useful for a start, but pay you less than they charge the client.

If you approach a publisher cold in the hope of getting literary translations, submit a sample of your work. For commercial or technical translations, advertise locally or put your name and details down in the reference department of the local library; prepare a short description of what you have to offer, have it photocopied or even printed, and distribute it to local factories and offices, particularly those with an overseas market.

Charge per thousand words, or on a time basis if the work is fragmented (lists, indexes, catalogues).

The **Translators Association** (a group for literary translators within the Society of Authors, 84 Drayton Gardens, London SW10 9SB) offers its members legal and general advice and assistance on matters relating to their work (but not the getting of it), on fees and the vetting of contracts.

The **Institute of Linguists** (24a Highbury Grove, London N5 2EA) can advise its members on rates and methods of charging, and can also give general advice and information; jobs are advertised in its journal.

language teaching

You can offer to give conversation classes in small groups. Charge for a series of classes—say, six to eight weeks in advance. It is not a good idea to work on a pro rata basis: sometimes after one session, some pupils back out of a seemingly firm commitment. Make clear the approximate standard of knowledge you expect of the group members (beginners, intermediate, advanced); possibly run separate classes for the different standards.

One-to-one tutoring can be for conversation or preparing pupils for exams or for going abroad. Get in touch with a firm or business with overseas connections and offer to coach individuals being sent to the foreign country. You may be paid by the sponsoring body, on a retainer basis. Such teaching may entail evening lessons to fit in with a pupil's working hours.

music teacher

If you are a good player with the requisite grades, you can teach the basics of your instrument at home to young children, or give lessons to someone who just wants to play better without aiming for a series of exams. A more unusual instrument has a rarity value—but potential pupils may be rare, too.

You may have to take pupils in the evenings, to suit them. Use a separate room where misplaced notes will not bring complaints from family or neighbours. There is no capital outlay—pupils will provide their own instrument (except for the piano which, if a pianist, you presumably already have). Sheet music and books of music are expensive; let the pupils provide their own or pay you for them. Do not photocopy music—it is likely to be an infringement of someone's copyright.

Inform your insurance company, in case your policy needs to be extended to cover any extra risks or liability.

Music teaching leading to grade examinations is a profession, not to be undertaken lightly by amateurs who may over-estimate their competence. A professional teacher needs to be responsible for lesson planning and a constructive long-term scheme for tuition, appropriate to each pupil.

Private teachers with professional music qualifications can join the **Incorporated Society of Musicians** (10 Stratford Place, London WIN 9AE). Under very exceptional circumstances, teachers without the necessary qualifications but with high reputations and considerable experience may be eligible to join. The Society makes recommendations of minimum fees to be charged for private tuition and makes available to its members advice and information which will consolidate their professional standing. Members of the private teachers' section are listed in the ISM's professional register of private teachers, which is distributed widely in the UK.

teacher

To coach potential exam candidates in your subject, you need to know the requirements of the different examination levels, and the curricula. Even without formal teaching qualifications, someone with specialist knowledge can be a tutor.

To find students, put a notice in the local paper, on newsagents' boards, at schools and colleges, churches, library, music and dramatic societies, and places where parents of young children or teenagers are likely to gather. You might even try the swimming pool, skating rink, sports clubs, leisure centre.

Charge per hour or series of lessons, and according to the standard required or level of exam.

Relative strangers coming constantly to your premises may affect your insurance cover, particularly for theft.

by correspondence
You may prefer tutoring at a distance rather than face to face.

The **Council for the Accreditation of Correspondence Colleges** (27 Marylebone Road, London NW1 5JS) will provide a list of accredited colleges, including an outline of the courses offered. The **Association of British Correspondence Colleges** (6 Francis Grove, London SW19 4DT) will send a list of its member colleges, with subjects taught. Write to the colleges doing courses in your subject and offer your services. There are not many vacancies for tutors except in the less usual subjects.

When applying, list your qualifications and experience and say why you think you will make a good tutor and how many hours you can give per week. If you are accepted, the college gives instruction on how to mark and grade the students' papers and the type of criticism to give. You are paid for the number of papers marked or students tutored, at rates varying with the subject and standard. The college reimburses you for postage.

typing

If you can type fast, accurately and with correct spelling, buy (or rent or hire) a good quality machine, preferably electric at least, possibly electronic, that has a daisywheel with plenty of alternatives and special symbols. Both with golfballs (now slightly on the decline) and daisywheels, there are many typefaces and styles to choose from and they are fairly quick and easy to change.

Daisywheel typewriters not only have different typestyles but can do different numbers of characters to the inch at the touch of a button.

It can be a bore to allow your customers to choose a typestyle and it often will not matter to them, but prepare a sheet of different ones for them to look at if they want to, so that they have the opportunity to choose—and so that you can match up work that has been half-completed by someone else.

If your spelling is good (and it needs to be, to be a home typist), acquire an audio machine (dictating machine) with footpedal and earphones. You can then transcribe letters, interviews, books, conferences. Make sure that your client uses the particular cassette that your machine will take—or vice versa.

To get work, advertise your services widely—on student noticeboards at the university or colleges; by a handout to local businesses and societies, radio station, consultants, barristers' chambers; by advertisements in literary publications. Advertise in professional trade journals, such as those for estate agents, solicitors, accountants, who always need typists. State exactly what you offer and how much you charge. Prepare samples of your work (letters, notices, plays, reports) to show prospective customers.

Try to get your name on the record at publishers and literary agents; long jobs such as typing a book are a good standby. To advertise in *The Author*, the journal circulated to the members of the Society of Authors (84 Drayton Gardens, London SW10 9SB), you have first to provide two references and a sample of your work.

Charge per thousand words or per sheet of paper or by the hour. Manuscripts, heavily corrected work and tabulated work will take longer, so scale your charges accordingly. Charge for the paper and any carbon paper used. Paper is heavy so try not to have to use the post for delivering your finished work.

Check whether the client expects you to tidy up grammar and correct spelling—some hate you to touch a comma.

You will have to be prepared to type for many hours on end, often about subjects that do not interest you. Take on only what you are sure you can complete; other people's typing may be uninteresting to you, but to them it is vital to have it back by the set time and perfectly typed. Much of the work will be rush jobs, left by the author/producer to the last moment, so be careful not to take on more than you can manage within the deadline set.

Once you have accepted work, complete it—if necessary, staying up until three in the morning—and learn the lesson not to take on too much the next time.

through an agency

If you hope to get work through a typing agency, do not offer to do work at home without having a decent typewriter; be prepared and take a sample of work done on it when you register at the agency.

Anyone employed by an agency should be regarded as an employee, and tax and national insurance deductions made by the agency. When someone who is self-employed works for an agency, the agency is still obliged to deduct national insurance from their payment, and, if they are in any doubt, will deduct tax, too. As a self-employed person, you may be able to reclaim any tax overpaid; national insurance contributions are payable anyway on the amount you earn so are usually not due for refund.

Do not ring up for work except when you are free of other commitments and thoroughly organised for it. If you are offered work and refuse it more than once or twice, even if your work is very good you are unlikely to be offered any again. Agencies do not like wasting time on trying people who keep saying 'no'.

If you have a genuine reason—such as a child getting ill, a death in the family—for being unable to complete the task, be willing to deliver the rest of the job to someone else whom the agency may find to take over from you.

as an agency

To run a typing agency yourself from home by sending out work to others to type in their own homes, you need to apply and pay for a licence from the regional office of the Department of Employment. (The licence fee is £114 a year.) It is against the law to operate such an agency without the licence, and against the law for an agency to advertise without making it clear that it is an agency. The Employment Agencies Licensing Section of the Department of Employment (2–16 Church Road, Stanmore, Middlesex HA7 4AW) can be asked for information and the address of your regional employment agency licensing office where application should be made.

word processing

If you can offer word processing, there is considerable scope for work at home. The cost of adequate equipment is high, but instead of buying a machine outright, you could lease one.

If you are relatively new to word processing, it is worth paying to get trained really properly: do not rely on picking up the skill from the manual supplied with a machine because this may not be sufficiently detailed or lucid. Word processors can be remarkably versatile and may be able to carry out tasks you did not know about.

The services you offer will depend on what hardware you have (a micro-computer, or a dedicated word processor which usually can handle a job faster and more easily) and what software (that is, the computer program) is available to you. If you have none of these when you are beginning, be sure to consult a reputable dealer with a proven back-up and maintenance service. The dealer will need a full description of the tasks you expect the equipment to perform so that he can advise you properly on the appropriate hardware and software: for instance, if you intend to process lengthy manuscripts, you will need a machine with considerable memory capacity, and preferably twin disk drives. For professional work, it will be almost essential to have a daisywheel printer rather than a dot matrix printer to give your finished work the first-class typewriter quality necessary for letters, manuscripts, theses, translations. It may be worth investigating the compatibility of word processing equipment with typesetting machines.

Make sure you ask about the loan of equipment if yours breaks down. Manufacturers' guarantee periods tend to be short—often only three months—and investing in a service agreement, although costly, may be prudent: if the machine breaks down in the middle of a job, you will need service quickly.

Do not forget to insure such expensive equipment specifically.

getting the work
Contact local employment agencies and typing bureaux; they will use your services if they do not have their own word processor, particularly if you prove reliable.

Small concerns may be pleased to have someone to sort information for their prospectuses or catalogues, sales lists or abstracts (for which you will need a 'sort' program on your software).

Another way to sell your word processing services would be to approach local societies, shopkeepers and small companies with an offer to compile their mailing lists and reproduce their mailshots (in which case, you will need software with a mailer). Holding a mailing list on disk—with membership fees, dates of renewal, special interests, for example—may seem expensive to the client initially but is invaluable when he needs 5000 labels produced within a day.

The Data Protection Act 1984 regulates the use of automatically processed information relating to individuals. Anyone who processes (for example, using a computer) personal data for business or professional purposes now has to register details of the information used and how it is obtained and disclosed. Explanatory booklets and application forms for registration are available from the **Data Protection Registrar**, Springfield House, Water Lane, Wilmslow, Cheshire SK9 5AX (telephone 0625 535777). The fee is £40, valid for a register entry for up to 3 years.

A word processor is useful for typing curricula vitae (CVs). Young doctors, for example, change jobs and need their CVs updated quite frequently: doing a six-month stint a few times as part of their post-graduate training, they need the details of each work period added to their CV afterwards, before they go on to the next. Charge a minimum rate for a CV, and then charge by the hour if it takes longer than you have allowed for in your minimum (say, half an hour). Get clients to write the facts out clearly and in the order in which they want them typed.

Establish how many redrafts of any text the client will need and how you will charge for them. You must be willing to correct your own errors without charge.

Although the use of a word processor cuts time and labour in completing an overall task, word processing is itself a time-consuming business so, when submitting estimates to clients, bear in mind the complexity of the job and the number of hours it will take as well as the materials and equipment used.

Be prepared to have to work at all hours of the day or night to meet deadlines. Although word processing is quiet, the printing-out is not.

doing work at home for an employer

Many of the people who work at home for an outside employer are doing the type of work generally done in a factory—assembling anything from watch straps to fire extinguishers, making toys or lampshades, filling Christmas crackers, finishing textile products. A lot of such work is done for the clothing industry. Much of the work is repetitive, requires little skill (but attention) and does not lead to the satisfaction of seeing the finished product. Women who had reached a highly skilled grade in factory work are sometimes asked to do work at home of a more specialised nature than the normal type of homework, and get much better rates of pay.

'New technology' homeworking can be done by someone with the relevant experience providing office-type services from home by the use of computers and word processors. These services include data base management, viewdata editing apart from word processing, programming, using equipment supplied by the employer. The range of equipment that may be used includes terminals attached by modems to the telephone network and through to the employer's computer; terminal adapted with microfiche reader; micro-computers, word processors and micro-writers. The telephone is a major piece of equipment.

Other types of outwork, such as typing, addressing envelopes, data preparation, invisible mending, are done on an agency basis for a freelance agent or for a firm or shop.

getting the work

There are no employment agencies specifically for outwork. It can often be found through friends and relations, and through having worked previously in a workshop, factory or office.

If you are thinking of doing this kind of work without existing personal contacts, the best places to look are the job columns in your local newspaper, notices in jobcentres, advertisements in magazines and on newsagents' boards. Ignore advertisements requesting payment for sending directories of homework or lists of employers: most are useless and some have been found fraudulent.

Some employers request a 'token of goodwill' or an agency fee before sending the first homework job. These, too, are better avoided. Do not send any money. Some sharp operators, realising that there is an overwhelming demand for homework, have cashed in on other people's need, and the promised work or payment never materialises.

If you do find acceptable homework, try to negotiate about the volume and regularity of work, and find out before committing yourself what the work involves in the way of equipment and materials. You may be expected to store bulky containers of stuffing for toys or plastic foam for packaging, to use flammable and/or nasty-smelling adhesives or paints, to leave awkward articles around the room to dry, to work with irritant substances or a noisy machine. Knives and other sharp instruments or poisonous substances will be a hazard if there are young children in the household.

Homeworkers are not excluded from the protection of the Health and Safety at Work Act 1974. Suppliers of homework have a duty to ensure as far as is reasonably practicable that you are not exposed to risks and to provide you with adequate information, instruction and training to help prevent this. If you have any doubts or complaints about health and safety matters related to your work, get in touch with the local office of the Health and Safety Executive or the environmental health department of your local authority. But before getting in touch with them, try to sort things out with the employer supplying you with the work. If you are in a trade union and there is a safety representative at the employer's factory, ask him or her for advice.

You could run into difficulties with the environmental health department of the local authority if there is a complaint that you create a 'nuisance'—for instance, by the use of an industrial sewing machine or other noisy equipment. Neighbours may be less tolerant of noise or fumes than the homeworker. It has often been via a complaint of this sort that a homeworker has discovered rules he or she was unaware of in a tenancy agreement which restricts the right to work at home, or that planning permission is required for changing the use of the premises. But many local authorities have adopted a more tolerant and helpful attitude to homeworking. Tenancy agreements, for example, have been altered to permit homeworking, and advice is available on such problems as noise prevention.

employment protection

Homeworkers as such are not included in the legislation incorporated in the Employment Protection (Consolidation) Act which gives entitlement to redundancy payment, maternity pay, compensation for unfair dismissal. In order to prove a claim to any of these payments a homeworker would have to establish employee status before a tribunal. The number of hours worked is important: a part-time worker who has been working less than 16 hours a week is not qualified to get redundancy payment or to claim unfair dismissal. But someone who has worked for more than 8 hours a week for an aggregate of 5 years or longer for the same employer does qualify for statutory rights.

Some local authorities lay down rules in their contracts with firms using homeworkers to ensure fair treatment of the homeworkers.

pay

In most cases, the pay for outwork is decided by direct individual negotiation with the supplier. Rates of pay vary widely and there are no hard and fast rules. It is worth remembering that there are hidden costs to homework besides the inconvenience of using the home as a surrogate factory and warehouse. Industrial sewing machines or other equipment needed may be expensive to run (and if not supplied, cost a lot to buy) and employers often take it for granted that homeworkers will supply smaller items like needles and thread. It is vital to take these extra costs into account in any negotiations.

Collection and delivery of work can be costly and inconvenient. Try to get the employing firm to do this for you, or at least to reimburse you.

Outwork is usually paid for on a piece work basis: a certain amount for each complete article or series of articles. The result is that many homeworkers are unaware of what they are paid for an hour's work. To avoid slaving for next to nothing, do a simple check: give the job your complete attention for an hour (allowing a little for the improvement you may make with practice) and see how much or how many you have achieved in that time. Then calculate your hourly rate of pay by multiplying the amount paid to you per unit of work completed by the number you can make in an hour. For example, if you are paid £1 for every 10 items (i.e. 10p each) and can complete six in an hour, the hourly rate is 60p. This does not take account of your overheads.

A fast worker will obviously earn more than a slow worker; an average worker should be able to earn at least the minimum rate, where this is set by statute.

wages councils

Wages councils were established for specific trades under the Wages Councils Act. They include clothing manufacturing, millinery, made-up textiles, bespoke tailoring, toy manufacturing.

The main function of a wages council is to fix the legal minimum wage to be paid by employers, either generally or for any particular work, and other terms and conditions of employment. The wages paid by an employer in a trade covered by a wages council must be adequate to cover any necessary expenditure incurred by the worker in connection with the employment. If they are not, the employer must refund the expenditure.

In 1987, the minimum rates for adults set by wages councils ranged from about £1.90 an hour to about £2.20 an hour. A homeworker is entitled to the same minimum rate of pay as other types of worker, and is also entitled to an allowance to meet additional costs—for example, for heating or lighting.

The terms and conditions established by wages councils must be observed by all employers of the workers concerned and are enforceable at law. A leaflet of guidance for employers and workers on the main changes made by the Wages Act 1986, with a list of the wages councils and the address of the regional wages inspectorate offices, can be obtained from the Department of

Employment **Wages Inspectorate**, 93 Ebury Bridge Road, London SW1W 8RE. Any worker who thinks he or she is not receiving the minimum rate of pay or conditions due under the Act should complain to the nearest wages inspectorate.

There are wages inspectors throughout the country; they can make an employer pay the full legal minimum rate and also pay any arrears that have built up from work already done. Complaints are investigated confidentially: the wages inspectors will approach your employer as if it were a routine visit (which they have to make anyway from time to time).

organisations for homeworkers

There are now several homeworking associations up and down the country. They bring homeworkers together as well as being able to offer advice and help, and pressing for improvements. There are homeworking associations or homeworking officers in various boroughs in London and elsewhere; your local authority offices, or a citizens advice bureau, may be able to tell you whom to contact. The **National Unit on Homeworking** (3rd floor, Wolverley House, 18 Digbeth, Birmingham B5 6BJ) can be asked for information about local associations. Some of these (for example, the London Wide Homeworking Group, the Leicester Outwork Campaign) produce a free 'Fact Pack' for homeworkers, and a newsletter or other publications on the subject of homeworking.

Trade unions organise workers in many trades where homeworking is common. Being together in a trade union is often the best way for workers to get improvements in pay and conditions. To find the trade union for your type of work, get in touch with the **Trades Union Congress** (Congress House, Great Russell Street, London WC1B 3LS) or the Low Pay Unit.

The **Low Pay Unit** (9 Upper Berkeley Street, London W1H 8BY; telephone 01-262 7278) is a research and campaigning organisation who can advise you on wages and employment rights, but will not be able to help you find work.

using an existing skill

Previous knowledge and experience by way of a hobby can be turned into a money-making activity. The gifted amateur can exploit his existing aptitude by working at home, using his skill and interest in an organised way for profit.

It is important not only to establish but to maintain a high standard for your work: the 80th teddybear must be just as well made and attractive as the first; your 50th quiche as firmly set and flavoured as the two you made for your first party.

getting better at it

Before commercialising your hobby, interest or skill, you should ensure that it is of a high enough standard. For instance, hand-made objects need particularly high standards of design, style, quality and execution: people who buy handmade objects are generally discriminating and looking for things that are beautifully conceived and carefully made.

For most skills, there are books giving practical hints and advice on how to make/produce/maintain/mend/restore whatever it is you are concerned with. Go to your local library and ask for a bibliography or look in the index or on the shelves for your particular subject and borrow copies of the most relevant titles.

The do-it-yourself and handyman magazines are an unending source of hints and explanations on practical activities, and there are magazines and journals covering most technical and professional occupations which it could be worth subscribing to, even if only for a short time before you get established. These may also provide you with possible sales outlets, through advertisements or articles. Consult *Willing's Press Guide* in the library to find out what is being published in your line and by whom.

Ask at your local library about any courses in the area. Many colleges of further education and polytechnics run courses for people who are thinking about going back to work or starting a new career. The courses are short (usually one day a week for ten weeks) and you need no qualifications to apply.

You may find that your local education authority is running a course which could help you to earn money in some way, even if that is not the primary purpose of the course. Adult education courses run by a local authority may be in the daytime or evening, and there is generally a very wide range of subjects. People's motives for taking courses vary, so try to make sure that you join a class where the others are likely to be serious students who want to learn more about the subject and are not there just for fun.

The **Workers' Educational Association** runs courses throughout the country on a varying range of subjects. The head office of the WEA (Temple House, 9 Upper Berkeley Street, London W1H 8BY) can let you have the name and address of the appropriate district secretary, who can provide details and a prospectus of courses in your area.

The **City and Guilds of London Institute** is an independent body, providing qualifications based on tests and examinations in a wide range of subjects. City and Guilds certificates are accepted as evidence of the achievement of recognised standards in technical skills. The sectors for which City and Guilds certificates are available include horticulture, creative studies, computing and information technology, furniture, catering, textiles, tourism and recreation. Courses preparing for City and Guilds qualifications are provided by colleges of further education, schools and training centres. Many of the courses are on a part-time basis; some full-time and evening courses are also available. Any technical college, the careers advisory service or local education authority office can provide information about City and Guilds courses available in the locality and about arrangements for enrolment. The Institute publishes an annual *Handbook* giving information about all the courses and services offered, and a list of publications and examination subjects. These are available free of charge from the City and Guilds of London Institute, 76 Portland Place, London WIN 4AA.

The 30 designated polytechnics in England and Wales offer an extensive range of advanced further education courses leading to the award of a variety of degrees, diplomas, certificates and professional qualifications. Normally, an A-level entrance qualification is required, but this standard may be waived or modified for mature students. The *Polytechnic Courses Handbook*, describing the full-time and sandwich advanced courses, is published annually by the **Committee of Directors of Polytechnics**; the 1988/89 edition costs £9 from the CDP (Kirkman House, 12–14 Whitfield Street, London WIP 6AX), and is also available for reference in public libraries. The CDP issues a free leaflet summarising full-time and sandwich courses. Details of part-time courses are given in the prospectuses and other literature issued by individual polytechnics.

Many people who cannot go out to study could work on a course at home. It is possible to study many subjects through a correspondence college. The **Council for the Accreditation of Correspondence Colleges**, an independent charity officially recognised by the Department of Education and Science, provides a list of accredited correspondence colleges (available from 27 Marylebone Road, London NW1 5JS). The Council will advise on particular courses and on correspondence education in general. The **Association of British Correspondence Colleges** (6 Francis Grove, London SW19 4DT) will send a list of its member colleges and the subjects they cover and also offers a free information and advisory service on aspects of correspondence education.

residential courses

If you can afford more time than for local further education classes, you may profit from a concentrated course at a residential college or centre.

Short residential courses are run for WI members by the **National Federation of Women's Institutes** at Denman College, Marcham, Abingdon, Oxon OX13 6NW. These include courses on practical skills and crafts, on marketing for pleasure and profit, on starting a small business. There are always more applicants than places.

A list of the residential courses for adults in various continuing education centres throughout the country, with the names and addresses of the organisers and some of the fees, is given in a booklet published twice a year by the **National Institute of Adult Continuing Education**, 19B De Montfort Street, Leicester LE1 7GE; price £1.15 for each of the booklets. The 80 or so topics covered by the courses include: beekeeping, bookbinding, botanical illustration, porcelain restoration, computers, cookery, crafts (from knitting to metalwork), dressmaking, furniture restoration, glass engraving, jewellery, painting and drawing, patchwork and embroidery, photography, picture framing and restoration, pottery, spinning and weaving, upholstery, woodwork, writing.

For example, West Dean College, Chichester, West Sussex PO18 0QZ, runs weekend and 5-day courses in creative and practical subjects for both beginners and those with more experience; at The Old Rectory, Fittleworth, Pulborough, West Sussex RH20 1HU, weekend and 4-day or 7-day courses are run on a range of practical subjects, including antique furniture restoration, beekeeping, machine knitting.

cooking

Unless you are already quite experienced at cooking, baking, sweet making, for family or friends, you should not consider making money out of doing so for other people.

The three main categories of cookery for other people are

making things (cakes, pies, jams, sweets, bread) for sale; providing meals, teas, coffees, snacks, for people to eat in your home; preparing dishes at home for other people's parties, dinners, lunches, receptions.

If you want to develop or perfect your skill, you could do an advanced cookery course at a local adult institute or take a course at a technical college for one of the City and Guilds catering, cooking or bakery examinations. If a WI member, you may be able to get on one of the Women's Institute's week or weekend residential courses at Denman College in Oxfordshire. There are more advanced sophisticated cookery courses costing several hundred pounds (for example, in London at the Cordon Bleu Cookery School and at Leith's School of Food and Wine); for some courses, there are long waiting lists.

There are statutory requirements under the Food Hygiene (General) Regulations 1970 (SI 1172; HMSO, £2.60) about the preparation and sale of food to be consumed by the public. The principal requirements relate to the cleanliness of the premises and equipment used, the hygienic handling of food, the temperatures at which certain foods are to be kept, the provision of water supply and washing facilities, the disposal of waste materials, the premises used for the purposes of a food business. Also there are numerous regulations under the Food Act 1984 applying to such things as labelling and composition.

If you let the environmental health department of your local authority know that you are intending to sell food to the public, before the scheme has gone past the initial idea stage, an environmental health officer will come to inspect your kitchen premises and equipment and storage facilities, and can make the necessary recommendations about complying with the appropriate legislation. He will be concerned about other domestic uses of a normal kitchen, such as washing of clothes, and about pets being allowed into the kitchen.

You should also consult your local planning authority in case you need planning permission for a change of use.

With any form of catering, there are food poisoning risks, particularly if handling delicate ingredients such as shellfish and the re-heating of precooked food. So, notify your insurers and arrange for public liability cover.

equipment and supplies

For cooking in quantities, you will probably need quite a lot of additional utensils, large dishes and extra gadgets; also aluminium foil or plastic film for covering and wrapping prepared dishes, and plenty of cool storage space. A big refrigerator will help; a freezer may be even more useful. You may find later that you need an extra cooker or microwave oven. Your fuel consumption will be high, so remember to cost this into the prices you charge. Also allow for the increased local authority rates you have to pay when rated as commercial premises.

Try to find a source for buying in bulk ingredients such as flour, sugar, dried fruit, and make use of catering packs of fats and jams, tea, coffee and cooking oil, and similar supplies.

Although you can save money by buying in this way, it may not be economic if you have to travel a fair distance to get to the appropriate cash-and-carry store or warehouse. You will need a large car or a van to transport the bulk packs you buy, and adequate storage space at home. Foodstuff is only worth buying in this way if you will be using it relatively quickly (before the bottom of a 10 kilo pack has gone stale or bad), and you must have somewhere to keep the containers of food dry and clean and at the right temperature for the contents.

The Grocer magazine publishes an annual marketing directory listing cash-and-carries geographically throughout the country and giving a list of food trade organisations. Ask for it in your library and also for the annual handbook of the National Federation of Fruit and Potato Trades, which gives information about wholesale fruit markets and lists their members and other relevant organisations.

for sale

Making cakes or confectionery or biscuits for selling through a local shop or cafe has the advantage that you can probably time the work to your own convenience—although, if successful, you may have to work hard to keep up with demand.

It would be a good idea to specialise in a particular line which other people are unlikely to make: unusual chutneys or pickles, lardy cakes, sweets or toffees or fudge, profiteroles or eclairs for filling, and seasonal fare such as simnel cake at Easter, yule log at Christmas, wedding cakes or birthday cakes. Home-made bread and rolls are always popular, even though more people nowadays make their own. So is other yeast baking—doughnuts, crumpets, croissants, danish pastries—which many women do not have time (or courage) to do themselves. Assess carefully how much time you are putting in so as to charge enough and make enough profit without pricing yourself out of the market.

Jams, jellies, chutneys, pickles, marmalade, mincemeat, are all likely to be good sellers, but some take a lot of preparing and processing. You need to have a reliable source of cheap fruit, either what you grow yourself or what you can pick at a nearby market garden or from friends' unwanted crops. Preserving sugar will be a major outlay, and you will need a supply of glass jars and tops. Labels should be attractive, and clearly marked with your name and address and the content of the jar (weight as well as description and date).

You may be able to rent a stall at a local market. Someone living in the country could become a shareholder in the Women's Institutes' market society (5p). You can then sell your goodies on the weekly market stall, charging the cost of making them plus a percentage; the WI gets a commission on the takings. Ask locally about a market in your area, or write to the **National Federation of Women's Institutes** (39 Eccleston Street, London SW1W 9NT; enclose a stamped addressed envelope) to find out where there are market societies. There are quite stringent requirements about the presentation and labelling of products to make sure that the statutory and the WI regulations are met. No prepared food that has been kept in a freezer may be sold at a WI market.

Whenever and whatever you are selling, it helps to display your produce attractively—in a basket or bowl, wrapped or in a labelled jar. Where possible, show your name and address (for repeat orders).

meals at home

If you are going to serve teas or refreshments or other meals in your home or garden, it is profitable to have a speciality such as 'olde englishe' teas, or traditional dishes. If you decide to do this on a more than occasional basis, you may need to obtain planning permission.

The English Tourist Board has a development guide *How to start a small restaurant or tearoom* (DG16; £3 from Department D, 4 Bromells Road, Clapham Common, London SW4 0BJ).

Ask whether a nearby stately home or castle, a local museum or gallery, the tourist information centre, guest houses and post offices, will put up a notice about the home-made food you offer. As well as advertising locally, you could try the publications of the regional tourist board, and any guide books or leaflets about the area.

The initial outlay for serving food in your house or garden will be for chairs, tables, crockery and tableware, table mats and cloths, napkins. Towels and soap for washbasins and lavatory paper are other items that will need constant replenishing and which you should try to buy in wholesale quantities.

You may have to provide car parking facilities and install extra lavatories and washbasins.

You must, by law, display the prices you charge for all items, from set teas to individual biscuits, and describe your products and ingredients accurately. When your turnover takes you over the VAT threshold, you will have to become registered and add the required percentage to the price of items consumed on the premises and to hot taken-away food. If you decide at any time to sell cigarettes, you will count as an 'excise trader' so that a customs officer has the right to come and inspect your premises (looking, for instance, for smuggled tobacco) at any time.

In Northern Ireland, anyone who provides food to be consumed on the premises by the general public has to meet the requirements of the Development of Tourist Traffic Act and be registered with the Northern Ireland Tourist Board and visited by the Board's inspectorate staff.

catering

If you are catering for business lunches, you can cook all the food at home and take it to the customers. You will need some suitable form of transport and, if you have to provide cutlery and plates, you need to be able to afford the original outlay—unless you can persuade the business firms that it is a good idea to have their own utensils.

When catering for special events—weddings, parties, lunches, dinners—you must plan properly and be disciplined about preparing in good time, as for a military exercise. It is a good idea to help out at big private or charity functions to see how things are organised and to get experience before you take on big parties yourself. You may need to get a like-minded friend (or two) to help with some occasions, for a fee or a share in the takings.

Consider early on if you want to stock up with tableware, china, glass and cutlery; having them to offer for hire with your catering services may help you to get the job.

Be prepared to offer alternative menus at different prices, and to do a breakdown and quote your charges at so-much per head. Remember to cost in your own time properly. It is a temptation, when you like cooking, to do it for love and to forget that your time should be profitably as well as agreeably used.

dressmaking

In order to make money from dressmaking, you must have a high professional standard. Many people want their clothes to have the individual fit, style and finishing that only a personal dressmaker can provide and they will expect a higher standard than from ready-to-wear clothes. Other people who will need you are the tall, the plump, and the unusual-shaped.

Courses on dressmaking and tailoring are available throughout the country at most centres of further education. A course for the City and Guilds certificate in clothing craft or in fashion could be useful. There are private schools who specialise in these subjects. In London, for instance, there is the Central School of Fashion, which offers three-month cutting and designing courses for gents' and ladies' clothing and children's clothing, courses in tailoring and light industrial sewing and in theatrical costume design and cutting; also special one-week revision courses for qualified students.

Specialist suppliers for the fashion clothing trade include R D Franks Ltd (Market Place, London WIN 8EJ) whose catalogue covers workroom equipment and magazines and books on dressmaking, pattern cutting, patchwork, embroidery, tailoring.

The advantage of this kind of work is that you need virtually no capital to start off with apart from a few tools—the sewing machine being the major item. Your sewing machine should have standard attachments for zips and gathering. A swing-needle action for buttonholes and overedging is helpful, and so is a reverse stitch for the ends of seams.

If you really want to make a success of this type of work, it would be wise to invest in an overlock machine. This will perform a neatening operation and will speed up the work output by about half but you will have to make quite a few garments to pay for it because these machines are relatively expensive.

Ideally, you should set aside one room for sewing only, with good lighting for your machine, a large cutting table, ironing board permanently up, dressmaker's dummy, hanging space for clothes and patterns, storage space for fabrics and trimmings. Keep leftover pieces of material graded by fabric and colour to make up packs of scraps to sell to patchwork enthusiasts. Equipment for pressing should include a steam iron, sleeve board and dressmaker's ham.

Your room for fittings should be private, and warm, and have a good mirror. Keep an appointments book.

This is a time-consuming way of earning money, and can be hard on the nerves if work has to be done in a hurry.

Cost your work at an hourly rate, and charge for all time devoted to the customer's needs—shopping, making, fitting. When estimating how much to charge, be clear whether it is you or the customer who supplies the fabric, lining, buttons, zips, and who does the shopping for them. If customers want to provide their own fabric and patterns, try to make sure that they supply a pattern which bears a fairly close resemblance to the finished article they want: otherwise, you can find yourself doing time-consuming and perhaps not totally satisfactory pattern alterations, and even complete re-designs. It can be helpful to keep a supply of pattern books handy, so that customers can show you what they want and you can make sure that they know what is involved in terms of quantity and types of material.

It helps both you and the customer to be able to give an estimate of time and cost at the outset. If a customer wants a rush job, do not accept it unless you can adjust your other work.

You may need to spend money on occasional advertisements, to supplement word-of-mouth recommendations.

theatrical costumes
Making theatrical costumes is different from ordinary dressmaking and needs a certain amount of experience or special

training, but anyone of reasonable intelligence and a capacity for speedy, hard-wearing work could find it fun to do even though not particularly well paid. For theatrical jewellery, hats and props needed for special productions, theatres are often on the look-out for extra helpers working at home. It is worthwhile contacting the wardrobe mistress of a local repertory theatre or well-established amateur companies, if only to do alterations to hired costumes.

alterations and repairs
Some shops and stores selling off-the-peg clothing to both sexes undertake alterations for their customers and make a charge for the service. These alterations are often done off the premises by private dressmakers and tailors. The work includes shortening or lengthening sleeves, hemlines, and trouser legs; taking in or letting out waists, skirts, trousers, and jackets; improving or adding surface stitching. It is quite a good idea to specialise in something like altering hems, while perfecting your skill in other directions.

Call on local shops and ask if you can do some alteration work for them. The sales assistant usually notes the alteration required and the shop may deliver and collect, or an arrangement could be made to visit the shop, say, twice a week.

Repairs are something different again: replacing zips, renewing pockets, replacing linings, changing buttons, strengthening broken seams, and invisibly mending holes. Dry cleaning shops are an outlet for this kind of work; shops may be willing to bring the work to you if you cannot collect it.

secondhand clothes

Selling good quality secondhand clothes (for adults or children), especially if you are able to offer an alteration service as well, could become a profitable business. You have to decide whether to buy outright from the people wanting to get rid of their garments and then sell at whatever price you choose or whether to sell on a commission basis, in which case it would be wise to stipulate a maximum length of time (for instance, three months) for which you will keep unsold goods. In all cases, you should stipulate that the clothes either are unworn or show minimum signs of having been worn, and are clean, freshly washed or dry cleaned. Be ruthless about rejecting anything that falls below your standard and style.

home machining

The clothing industry throughout the country uses many home-workers with dressmaking and tailoring abilities. Generally speaking, a home machinist is required only to machine the garments; the pressing, buttonholes, buttons and finishing are done by the manufacturer later.

You have to work very hard to make much money from this sort of work. Pay is generally by piece rates—that is, an agreed price per garment—with all the parts supplied cut and ready for machining together. Rates vary from manufacturer to manufacturer and with the quality and work content of each style. (The minimum rate of the wages council for clothing manufacturing works out at just over £1.98 an hour.) Standards in cheap garments are lower—no underpressing, fewer machine stitches per inch (or cm), no hand-sewing—and so are rates of pay.

The delivery is made in bundles. Bundles of the same style and colour offer continuity, and the best opportunity for profit to the machinist. Switching of colours and style entails thread changes, breaks in rhythm, and loss of time.

knitting

Knitting by hand and knitting by machine are two entirely different skills.

Machine knitting is much quicker than hand knitting and the coned yarns available for machine knitting are much cheaper than yarns for hand knitting.

There are machines which can produce a wide range of stitches and fabrics and use fine industrial yarns as easily as the fashionable chunky yarns. Usually a standard gauge machine that knits most thicknesses of yarn is the type for first-time knitters to opt for. Punch card and electronic machines make patterning simple, and designing your own stitch patterns is within most people's capabilities.

A number of adult colleges run courses on machine knitting, and anyone buying a new machine should be sure to get a comprehensive demonstration from the manufacturer's representative. Accredited correspondence courses are available from Metropolitan Sewing Machines (321 Ashley Road, Parkstone, Poole, Hants BH14 0AP), who also have a large mail order department for accessories, yarns, machines, patterns, books for machine knitters. They also run **To & Fro**, a postal knitting club, with a quarterly magazine covering all aspects of machine knitting.

You should, if possible, set aside a room for the machine and ironing board to be kept up, with plenty of storage space.

It is advisable to keep notes of the work you do, tensions, sizes of garments, yarns used, so that if repeat orders are placed, you can save time by just referring to the previous order. Make a rule to provide the yarn yourself – since you are knitting as a business, you will be able to make savings on the price of yarns by bulk buying.

A few sample garments in the first instance should be enough to start the ball rolling. Do not charge too little for the first orders in an effort to get started quickly: once you have sold one under-priced garment, it is difficult suddenly to increase the price. Work out a reasonable profit margin from the beginning.

hand knitting

Knitting on knitting needles is more versatile than machine knitting and can be done anywhere in the home, while journeying, watching sport or television. Although a knitting machine produces a complex fabric quite quickly, the individuality of hand knitting and the ability to interpret any pattern means that the end product may be original and attractive, hardwearing and practical.

Textured or fancy yarns hand knit particularly well. Aran patterns incorporating cables and raised stitch patterns are ideal, rather than Fair Isle which many machines can do very well.

Shops and spinners need hand knitters for testing sets of instructions and for producing display garments, but the pay, reckoned by the hour, is very low. Rates are related to the thickness of the yarn and the complexity of the pattern. Write direct to the spinners whose yarn you like and ask if they require anyone to test-knit for them. Each has a different entry test, and different requirements for making up the work—some prefer you to do it, others do not. But whoever you produce for will want clean work done at the correct tension (most important), so you will have to work with care and accuracy. There is also a small market for baby garments. The **British Hand Knitting Association** (POB CR4, Leeds LS7 4NA) can supply the names and addresses of the yarn spinners who are its members.

Some hand knitters find an outlet for their skills by doing freelance designing either for spinners or for placing in women's magazines or the women's pages of daily papers. Also, a few work in close collaboration with specialist spinners and colourists who need their fashion designs for the next seasons to be interpreted from their vaguely-described ideas into clear and concise instructions for the hand knitter to follow.

Many boutiques commission hand-knitted garments of high quality from outworkers, and provide the patterns and materials, and deliver and collect. You would need to negotiate a price per hour or per garment. Look for their advertisements or go into your nearest one(s) and offer your services.

When hand knitting or crocheting for an individual customer, you may not be able to charge a fully realistic price for the time spent. A lot depends on the complexity of the pattern but in order to bring the selling price to an acceptable figure, you may find that your notional pay per hour works out at under 50p.

photography

A skilful and experienced amateur photographer could specialise in portrait photography (babies, children, adults, animals), especially in a place where there is no photographic studio in the neighbourhood. Or go out to record local events such as weddings, birthday parties, parades, fetes, dances and other social or sporting occasions.

There are courses in photography at adult education institutes and colleges, including residential ones; some are specifically for a type of photography—landscape, colour, portrait. There is a City and Guilds certificate course in photography.

Quite a lot of paper work is involved, and an efficient filing and recording system is necessary. Set up a room to use as a dark room with all the necessary developing and printing equipment if you decide to do your own processing. Generally, black-and-white work can be undertaken in domestic surroundings with advantage in speed and cost, and possibly a better product. Colour is more difficult and demands a higher capital investment, so it is probably better to let a professional laboratory do it for you. A small local firm can generally produce the work more cheaply than you can do it for yourself.

For portrait photography, to get technically good results you will need a suitable room to use as a studio, and good lighting and equipment. Backgrounds are important: two or three rolls of different shades and colours of paper are useful. Provide a mirror in the reception area or waiting room.

You may need two or three cameras, to suit different types of subject, and a spare while one is being serviced or mended. Since lenses seldom go wrong, with interchangeable types it suffices to have one set of lenses and two bodies. Do not assume that you have to have the most expensive equipment—skilled use of a simple camera can be just as effective as the most elaborate apparatus (even if less impressive to the client). Subscribing to a photographer's journal (a subscription can be set against tax, as a business expense) will provide you with up-to-date information about latest technical developments; go to professional photographic exhibitions to get ideas.

Get your supplies of paper and films and other materials direct from the suppliers, on wholesale terms. If you link yourself to one of the big photographic firms, you may get a special discount in return for advertising their wares by your use of them.

A local art shop or gallery may be willing to display a notice about your services; estate agents or auctioneers may want photographs taken of what they are selling.

Put an advertisement in the local paper, and have printed cards to distribute. Make use of the announcement columns in the papers for new babies, future weddings, forthcoming anniversaries or special events. For weddings, make contact with the local vicar, ministers and register office; remember brides can come back for baby pictures.

It can be profitable to offer the finished photograph(s) in a special album or frame provided (and charged for) by you.

If someone commissions you to take a photograph, the copyright belongs to him. Although it is customary for you to retain the negative, you cannot use the photograph (say, for display) without his permission. And if you charge too much for extra prints, he may just get the original one copied.

A much-needed service would be to take close-up photographs of people's jewellery and small valuables for identification purposes, to be kept ready to support an insurance claim after a burglary. Each item must stand clear of any other item; you may need to take more than one view of some. Make sure that if the object has any identifying features, such as damage or distinctive marks, they are clearly visible and defined. Photograph small items with a 12-inch ruler or a matchbox or coin next to them, to give an indication of their true size. Number the prints and give the negatives to the owner.

An alternative line to supplement commissioned orders would

be to offer your photographs of suitable subjects or objects to publishers (newspaper or magazine), greetings card manufacturers or illustrated magazines for reproduction. Blockmakers work from black-and-white glossy prints or colour transparencies; they do not like reproducing from ordinary colour prints. Slides should not be mounted in glass: use plastic sleeves.

In general, photographs are sold to magazines on the basis of one reproduction right. However, although the copyright (and negative) remains the property of the photographer, it would be unethical, and in the long run inadvisable, to submit the same picture to another magazine in the same field, at least until several years had passed. If in doubt, tell the editor and let him decide.

When sending out your work, label each print clearly, identifying it as yours with your name, address and telephone number (and make a note of what you have submitted to whom). Type captions and fix them to the back of the print—do not write on the back of prints as the ink offsets onto the next print. If there is the slightest possibility of a picture being reproduced the wrong way up, mark clearly which is the top. Flower close-ups are particularly liable to be inverted. Send return postage to make sure of getting your work back.

Flat fees are more common than royalties for photographs. You may be asked to relinquish the copyright if the photographs are to be published in a book. If so, your fee should be higher. The important point is to know what you are selling and not to relinquish more rights than essential to ensure a sale.

With illustrated articles, most magazines pay by the page as published. An editor should tell you in advance what he will pay and you can then decide if it is worth your while.

Articles for magazines may need to be accompanied by photographs; you could offer to cooperate with an author and provide photographic illustrations. Keep on friendly terms with picture editors. They are often asked to suggest photographers for specialised subjects and can steer work your way.

repair work

You will in many cases have to invest not only in the cost of the materials used but spend a lot of your time and thought and skill in putting an article back into a near-perfect state. Your charge for each job must reflect this outlay as well as the visible (or invisible) restoration.

Even if you are not specifically asked, give an estimate of what you are going to charge when you accept an article for repair or restoration. This gives the customer the chance to withdraw rather than make difficulties after you have invested your time and money in the work.

You may be housing some quite valuable objects, and will need to keep them safe. You can insure for their loss or damage by fire while at your premises, or theft where there has been forcible entry, but not for unexplained loss or for damage you do while working on them. Even where you can get insurance, the problem of value arises: you only have the owner's word for it and, even quite innocently, many people are under the impression that their picture, clock, book, is worth a lot more than it really is. Theoretically, you should ask each customer for proof of value and authentication, but this is in most cases impracticable. Therefore, put a clear description in your register, such as 'Worcester coffee can' or 'Original photograph, about 1914: group of soldiers', with the customer's estimate of the value beside it. Then keep the register as far away from the articles as possible so that, in the event of fire, the two are not lost together.

The work you do will involve having other people's possessions left with you while you work on them or for repair (a picture to frame, a chair to re-upholster, a clock to mend), so give a ticket to make sure that the right thing will be collected by or on behalf of the right person. Be sure always to have the owner's or deliverer's name and address, or at least a telephone number, in case no one comes to collect at the appointed time. Some customers may forget that, or where, they have left an article for repair.

Perhaps it would be wise to ask for a deposit or payment in advance. In repair work, there is a greater risk of people failing to collect their possessions, and you would be left with the loss not only of the cost of the materials you used but of the time expended—which you are unlikely to be able to recover even if, eventually, you sell the uncollected object.

Once you are really good, make yourself known to insurance loss adjusters and assessors: they need to know where things can be repaired—it may be worth offering them a discount.

By law, under the Torts (Interference with Goods) Act 1977, you have to try to contact the owner or responsible person when you have been left with articles that have not been collected, but after making reasonable efforts to obtain instructions about the uncollected goods, you have the right to sell or dispose of an abandoned item. Before selling, however, you have to send in writing, by registered or recorded delivery post, due notice (in cases where money is owed, not less than three months) of the date on or after which you propose to sell. If large amounts are involved, get legal advice first.

bicycle repairing

With the increasing number of cyclists everywhere, if you are reasonably handy, it could be profitable to set up a bicycle repair business. This can be done without needing more than a cupboard for tools and spare parts, and a shed or a yard or other suitable space where you can dismantle and reassemble bikes. You may need to stable some bikes overnight or for a few days while working on them, so a lockable covered bicycle rack or a lock-up shed could be useful, too.

The tools required are relatively simple, plus oil, grease, paint, chrome cleaner, inner tubes and puncture repair equipment; some spare parts may be obtainable only from the bicycle's manufacturer.

Identify each bike carefully with its owner. Try to give some idea of how much you will charge for the job beforehand. Ask for a deposit, particularly if you are at all doubtful about the bike being claimed when ready.

Tell local schools, colleges and clubs, firms and factories, that you are offering this service; also put notices in papers, in shop windows and your own.

If you have the necessary skill (and sources of supplies), rebuilding and restoring old, broken-down bicycles for resale can be profitable.

book binding

To acquire sufficient knowledge and skill to do book binding or book restoring on a commercial basis, you must attend classes.

Courses are given at some polytechnics and schools of printing and technology, and there is a City and Guilds certificate in book binding and the special requirements of restoration and conservation of archive material. West Dean College (Chichester, West Sussex) offers a number of courses in book binding, including for those with some experience.

Books on the subject include *Basic book binding* by A W Lewis (£3.00, Dover Publications, distributed by Constable), *Introducing bookbinding* by Ivor Robinson (£12.95 from Peter Stockham, 16 Cecil Court, London WC2N 4HE) and the *Manual of Bookbinding* by A W Johnson (£5.95, Thames and Hudson). These give a good idea of the work involved, and could be used on their own as a guide or in conjunction with an adult education class.

Presses are expensive and a secondhand basic set of brass tools for lettering a book will set you back at least £25 (over £65 new) and you will need several of different sizes.

Do not embark on leather bindings until you have gained enough experience: poor workmanship is likely to affect the value of the book. It is the most expensive, but probably the most profitable area of book binding. Good leathers cost several pounds a square foot and you need to have a wide selection in order to match the materials you are asked to repair. Case binding in cloth, rexine or buckram (strong linen) is cheaper and easier to work.

Secondhand booksellers and dealers may welcome someone who can carry out anything from minor repairs to re-binding a book. Advertise locally and also in specialist or professional publications whose readers may want their reports, magazines or theses to be bound. Make sure to add return postage to your charge for any work you get by post.

Your charges must cover your overheads and your own time as well as the materials you use. Before spending too much time on a book which in itself is not worth more than a few pounds, get the customer's confirmation that he is willing to pay your price. Where there is a choice of material, you could discuss the possibility of using a cheaper one.

china repairing

China repair and restoration requires exceptional patience and an eye for detail, particularly in the moulding of replacements for missing pieces of porcelain. You need to have a gift for this painstaking, slow and complex work. Do not take on high quality work until you have gained adequate experience.

Details of some courses on china mending for beginners are available from Robin Hood's Workshop, 18 Bourne Street, Sloane Square, London SW1W 8JR. West Dean College (Chichester, West Sussex) has a one-year diploma course on the restoration of antique ceramics and porcelain, and there are short courses at other residential colleges in different parts of the country, such as The Old Rectory at Fittleworth, West Sussex.

You need good light to work by, with very good ventilation and freedom from dust and grease. After an initial outlay of around £500 for drill, air brush and compressor, the running costs for materials are moderate because only small quantities of materials are used. But you will need the best quality sable brushes; these do not wear well and are expensive to replace. The small knives, methylated spirits, contact adhesive you use, and the china being mended, should be kept safely out of the way of other members of the household, especially children and pets.

Try asking the local museum and antique shops and insurance loss adjusters whether they can put work in your way.

clock repairs and restoration

There is a shortage of repairers and restorers of clocks everywhere, and most craftsmen in this field have a waiting list of customers that in some areas can be as long as twelve months.

The costs involved in clock repairing are low. Special working space is not required and equipment is minimal: many of the tools (screwdrivers, file, small hammer, hacksaw, drill, emery cloth) are likely to be already in the toolbox of an average d-i-y household. You will need a small angled desk lamp to direct the light on your work as required—sunlight is too unreliable.

The main requirements for the clock repairer are manipulative skill, training, patience. The first requirement is met if you have any skill in metalwork, embroidery, woodwork, typing or any other task that has disciplined the hands and eyes. The second can be satisfied by taking one of the training courses that are available, and the last is not an extraordinary virtue.

Occasional courses in clock repair and restoration are given at some residential centres, such as The Old Rectory, Fittleworth, West Sussex. The **British Horological Institute** runs correspondence courses leading to the BHI examination in three grades of technical horology (preliminary, intermediate and final), each of one year's duration. For details of fees and syllabus, write to the BHI, Upton Hall, Upton, Newark, Notts NG23 5TE. Other technical colleges also have classes on clock making and repairing leading to the Institute's examinations. Horological enthusiasts may enrol as associate members of the BHI (subscription £26 a year plus £2 joining fee) without the need for examination procedures, and will get the *Horological Journal* monthly and be kept informed of recent developments and techniques. There are BHI branches throughout the country.

There are some craftsmen clockmakers who take beginners and those already partly experienced. These include Laurie Penman, Castle Workshop, 61 High Street, Totnes, Devon TQ9 5PB, who runs holiday courses and 'sandwich' courses throughout the year.

A holiday course is usually one or two weeks of individual instruction in the morning only. Enough can be learnt in the time about the cleaning of clocks and some of the simpler (and most frequently needed) adjustments, to discover whether this is the way you wish to earn money.

A sandwich course consists of periods of instruction interleaved with running your own workshop. After an initial course of two weeks, students may be able to set up their own business and begin to accept customers. Students can then return for further tuition, bringing with them any clocks that present them with problems. The cycle can be repeated until you achieve full competence. The advantage is that training is specific to requirements, it is never necessary to turn away a prospective customer because the work is beyond present expertise, and time is not wasted on skills that may never be needed. You can also gain some commercial experience on pricing.

The level of earning that can be made by clock repairing or restoration will vary with the district and the expertise of the craftsman. Repair charges are based on hours spent at the bench: the intricacy of each job and the time it takes will be the main criteria for the price to charge.

picture framing

To do picture mounting and framing to a professional standard, you need knowledge of what you are doing, skill, and a lot of space. The minimum area needed to work in and for storage of materials would be, say, that of a double garage.

Tools are expensive, particularly the implement for cutting mitred corners (without this, the corners will not be good enough—and a frame with wrong corners is not worth any money at all). You will also need a machine for cutting professional-looking mounts, unless you have the skill to cut them by hand.

To be able to offer to make any size and kind of mount and frame, you need a selection of mount boards, and of mouldings for each type of frame suitable for different styles of picture and a selection within each group (gold, plain wood, antique finish, metal and so on). Having a wide choice enables you to offer alternatives at different prices.

Coloured frames are now quite fashionable. It is possible to use different plain woods and paint or stain them to provide a variety of finishes—cheaper than trying to stock a wide choice.

Use 2mm glass. Glass comes in large sheets which are difficult to store, so get the shop to cut it into some standard sizes. Glass is quite tricky to handle; if you keep breaking large sheets, you would probably lose out on the whole endeavour. Hardboard, too, comes in large sheets (about 8ft × 4ft) which need to be cut to size.

Outside London, materials may not be readily available, and firms do not usually sell in small quantities, so some capital is needed to stock up. Before committing yourself financially, try to find out what demand there is in your area and whether people are prepared to pay an economic price.

Try advertising, and getting work through a local craft or book shop, art gallery, photographer, artists' group; tell architects and designers, advertising agencies, and local firms or institutions that you can do framing for them.

upholstery

Upholstery, or more specifically re-upholstery, especially of antique furniture, can be a well-paid and interesting way of earning money at home. However, your enjoyment and earning power will rest on how motivated you are and how much you are prepared to invest in time, money and energy. There is a wealth of difference between making an acceptable job of re-covering a tatty footstool in an old bit of brown dralon for a few £s and being able to restore an antique crinoline chair in a specially woven silk for a top market price. The latter is more interesting, more satisfying and work that is highly sought after and highly paid, yet possible to do in your own home.

Be prepared to spend some money on improving your skill. Invest in yourself and get some good training. Skilled upholstery cannot be learned from a book (use books for reference and reminders at a later stage). Find as many sources as you can, without relying on one teacher or one form of training.

Local authorities run upholstery classes at adult education institutes, in the daytime, or evening or weekend sessions. Also write to the **London College of Furniture** (41 Commercial Road, London E1 1LA) for information about their course in upholstery, designed for people who wish to run their own upholstery workshop and business. The course provides practical instruction in a wide range of modern and traditional styles of upholstery, tools and equipment, upholstery materials and soft furnishing fabrics and trimmings; also the basics of frame repair, wood finishing, furniture history and small business studies. The course can be taken full-time or part-time, and leads to a City and Guilds examination and certificate.

Regular weekend to four-day courses are run at The Old Rectory, Fittleworth, West Sussex and by some individual upholsterers in various parts of the country.

Try working for a while for a local upholsterer, who may be grateful for someone to come in and strip down furniture. Practise on your own furniture and on chairs bought cheaply at local auctions.

the workplace

It is possible to work in the middle of the home, but not for long. Something or somebody will have to give way to the lack of space, the amount of filth that comes out of old chairs, the stocks of goods and fabrics and the general disruption.

The ideal workplace would be to convert a shed, stable, barn or garage. Remember to think about heating it effectively: careful stitching of fine fabrics in January temperatures is impossible. A large and otherwise unused room in the house would do. It should be at ground floor level to have easy access for larger pieces of furniture. It is important to be able to shut the door at the end of a working day.

supplies

In order to buy at wholesale prices and make money by selling at retail prices, you have to invest your money in buying the large quantities offered by warehouses. Springs, for instance, usually come in bundles of 50, tacks are cheaper by the 10-kilo box, and webbing is usually sold in quantities of 4 or 5 large reels at a time. Get a loan, if necessary, to buy in what you need. If you charge sensible prices for your finished product, you will soon pay for your goods (and your loan).

Look in the Yellow Pages for upholstery warehousemen or go and ask other upholsterers where they get their supplies. Many textbooks on upholstery list suppliers at the back.

fabrics

Get in touch with one or two high-quality fabric suppliers. Explain that you are wanting to use their fabrics for quality re-upholstery work. You will be expected to choose and purchase pattern books of these fabrics to show your customers; if you are going to deal in quality fabrics, expect the books to cost anything up to £50 to £60 each. This outlay can be recouped on your first few pieces of work.

You may be working on too small a scale to make it worthwhile for suppliers to open a credit account for you. Instead, they may let you pay 'pro forma'—that is, you have to pay for the fabric before they deliver it but you pay the wholesale price. Ask the suppliers, or telephone local stockists, to find out the appropriate retail price to charge for the fabric. If your suppliers recommend a retail price, stick to it rather than lowering the price because it appears to you to be expensive.

The important thing is to keep to one or two suppliers to begin with, and do work for customers only in the fabric(s) you can provide.

pricing your work

The temptation is to undervalue your work because you are new at it, or because you feel that working from home is not a 'proper' business. You may be nervous of your customers, be they family, friends or strangers, and, above all, you may not be used to talking about, handling and demanding money for your own labours.

Do not mess about with sliding scales of charges for family and friends or for people you suppose cannot afford the price.

From the day you put that first advert in the local shop or take on your cousin's chaise longue, you must have thought out your pricing properly. It is no use spending days and maybe weeks on work that loses money—your time would be more constructively spent helping local charities.

Do not try to save your customers money. Offer them the very best quality you possibly can first, and then show them the alternatives.

Assuming you have taken the time, trouble and money to acquire a reasonable standard of skill, charge the going rate for the job. Telephone around locally or, if you feel embarrassed, use the Yellow Pages for areas farther afield to find out what others are charging and get a rough idea of what an acceptable price is for a job. If you find people are reticent and cagey about their prices, this may be because they have not worked this out properly themselves.

Charge the going rate first and then, when you are working, note how long the job takes and what materials you are using. It is not always sensible to charge by the hour: you could find yourself earning less as you get more skilled instead of more. It will help if you charge separately for labour and for materials in order to keep track of the costs.

a deposit
You may have to pay out a lot of money on materials long before you are paid for the work. Asking 30 per cent of the estimated cost in advance is not unreasonable. If the customer does not want to pay the 30 per cent, it may be a fair indication of his or her willingness and ability to settle the final bill.

getting help
You probably cannot do everything yourself: there is not the time and you may not be able to acquire all the necessary skills. So, look through the Yellow Pages, the local ads and ask around for people to help you with, for example, furniture repairing and re-polishing. Stripping down furniture is not a highly skilled job, and someone local may be glad to earn some money doing that for you while you do the skilled work.

If you cannot afford a carding machine or buttoning machine, you may be able to find a local upholsterer who would be willing to hire out the machines or do the work for you.

Do not waste time driving around in a van and going to weight-lifting classes in the evening—get yourself a driver and mate who can see to deliveries and collections and who will be sensitive to the value of the furniture and the needs of your customers.

extending your options
Once you have become a skilled upholsterer, you need not always do the same work. Upholstery has so many trades allied to it that you can move on or do several things at a time. Options include furniture restoration; buying and selling antiques (especially upholstered pieces); selling fabrics and braids; making curtains, pelmets, lampshades, soft furnishings such as loose covers, bed covers. Another extension might be teaching upholstery at home, full-time, part-time, in the evenings, for weekend courses.

writing

In only a minority of cases will writing, fiction or non-fiction, earn the writer a reasonable income, whatever the intellectual rewards. You will be investing, as well as time and money, a great deal of emotional energy and you will have to be prepared for disappointment. Only one out of approximately every 500 manuscripts submitted to publishers and agents during a year will make it to the bookshop and library shelves. But do not despair if a first attempt is turned down—a large bottom drawer for the stowing away of rejected typescripts is a pre-requisite for the aspiring author.

Evolve some sort of filing system, and keep details of all work sent out, to whom, the date, the reply. And keep a careful note (and receipts) of any expenses that might be allowable for tax, such as paper, postage, fares, telephone calls, reference books.

The completion of a manuscript is only the beginning of the process of getting a book into print and, to start with, the writer will be paying out sums with no guarantee of their ever being recouped. As well as the cost of the stationery and postage incurred in submitting a manuscript, it will probably be necessary (unless you are an accurate and competent typist) to pay for the services of a professional typist to make a fair version and subsequently you will probably also have to pay for photocopies.

presentation

Although the worth of a book should shine through however badly presented it is, publishers and agents are only human and are therefore much more likely to be sympathetic towards a manuscript which looks as though it has had care lavished on it and is new and unhandled, rather than one which has obviously been around most of the publishing houses already.

Generally, publishers will only accept a manuscript if it is typed, preferably double-spaced and on A4 paper, with minimum corrections. If a typescript has been sent out and returned from several publishers, the first few pages inevitably become rather dog-eared and it would be worth having these retyped or photocopied. A good solid binder will ensure that the pages remain in order and make their handling easier.

submitting your work

Before sending out anything (perhaps even before you begin to write), study the market to discover where to send your work.

Take time to look round your local bookshop or library to get an idea of which publishers deal with which type of book. You can normally tell from jackets and blurbs what books are similar in type to yours, and therefore which publisher is most likely to be interested. It is a waste of everyone's time to send a scientific manual to a children's publisher, and vice versa.

When first approaching an agent or publisher, mark the envelope for the attention of the manuscript department or the fiction or non-fiction editor, as appropriate. If you are going to send it to a named editor, do make sure that that person is still working at that company and that he or she is still the relevant person for your work.

Publishers and agents prefer, and some insist on, having an initial letter from a writer describing the work, with a synopsis and possibly a sample chapter to show the style of writing. If impressed by this, they will ask to see further chapters or the whole manuscript. Remember that an editor or agent receives dozens of letters about manuscripts every week, so try to make yours stand out. The most effective way is also the simplest—just stick to the bare facts about the kind of book you have written and are trying to interest someone who knows nothing about it, or you, to read. Personal detail should be kept to any relevant experience in writing professionally or your connections with the subject matter of the book. Again, presentation is important: a badly handwritten letter on a scrap of paper torn from an exercise book will not go down well.

You need to be patient while waiting for a response from a publisher to your typescript once they have asked to read it after your preliminary letter. It is likely to take months rather than weeks to get a reply. Most publishers send an acknowledgement slip when they receive a manuscript; if you want to make sure that they will, enclose a self-addressed envelope. It is always a good idea to include return postage anyway—if you are lucky, it will never be needed. If you think the publishers or agents are being an unconscionably long time in coming back to you, write or telephone and then, if you think you are wasting your time with them, drop them a note asking for immediate return of the manuscript. Publishers and agents are for the majority of their time concerned with their already published clients and the new, unsolicited writer is not a high priority for them.

Do not send an agent or publisher copies of rejection letters you have received from other firms. However gracious the rejection letter may appear to you, these are all too often just form letters and will be recognised as such by another publisher or agent. The other reason is that publishers are clannish people and will be influenced by the fact that a colleague in another company has turned the book down.

Some firms send you a reader's report. This can be useful if, in the light of the comments, you feel that you should rewrite the work. If they do not send a report, it is unlikely that you will get any more detailed comments than those that accompany the returned manuscript. If you feel that your manuscript has not been adequately read, there is no point in re-contacting that firm—try again somewhere else.

literary agents
A literary agent represents a writer and, in return for 10 per cent

(or more) of any money made for the writer by the agent, looks after the writer's interests. If a first-time writer is lucky and his book is accepted by an agent, the agent may well give some advice about possible rewrites, based on his or her experience of what publishers are looking for.

An agent will have a clearer idea of which editor in which publishing house would be interested in your work; the publisher may be more willing to consider the book seriously if it has been sent to them by an agent. Most importantly, if the publisher does accept the book, the agent is in a better position than the writer to negotiate a financial deal.

An agent understands the terms and jargon involved in drawing up a contract and what loopholes and traps to look out for. Within an agency, there may be a separate department solely devoted to the selling of subsidiary rights—that is, translation, american, serialisation, film, television rights.

on acceptance

When the publishers have accepted your book and you have accepted their contract, the process of editing will occur. You may be asked to expand the text. If, alternatively, the publishers ask you to cut, they normally give you guidelines as to what the most suitable cuts would be. They may also suggest areas where they feel that action or characterisation needs strengthening or clarifying.

Once a book has been accepted and the contract signed, you will still have to be patient: it normally takes about a year to 18 months before publication actually takes place.

contract and rights

The contract, or agreement, signed by both the publisher and the writer, binds both sides to various commitments. Publishers have their own individual contract forms, which can be changed to suit the circumstances of different books and writers. On the whole, these are fair and equitable, but remember that they are for the protection and advantage of the publisher. Publishers are not going to try and do one of their authors down (this would make the whole process self-defeating) but they want to make as much profit as possible from the book.

Never assign the copyright in your work. A publisher simply needs an exclusive licence to publish the book.

The major things to look out for are exactly what rights you are selling to the publisher for the advance and royalties he offers to you and that the publisher undertakes to publish the book within a specified time. If you are dealing through an agent, he or she will try to ensure that the publisher has the right only to sell the book in the english language in the UK and british commonwealth. The USA, foreign language editions, serialisation, film, television, radio and play rights and adaptations are all separate entities and should, ideally, each be exploited separately to the writer's best advantage.

On the whole, books are first published in hardback, probably not in very large quantities (5000 is a fair first print run), and then go into paperback. The hardback publisher normally controls paperback rights and the writer will receive a percentage of the sum negotiated between the hardback and the paperback publishers (in some cases, this is the same or a sister company). This percentage varies, but should always be above 50 per cent in favour of the writer. In the same way, if the publisher also buys the subsidiary rights, the writer will receive a percentage of any money the publisher makes from the re-selling of them.

Ensure as far as possible that the publisher is obliged to receive your consent, after consultation, about the sale of any rights in the book beyond the original hardback publication and that the publisher generally keeps you informed about the fate of the book.

Apart from making sure what rights you are giving to the publisher to handle, you should check what the circumstances are under which a contract may be terminated, leaving you free to resell the rights (the copyright in the book remains with the author: if you were to sell the copyright, you disclaim all ownership and your work could be used again and again without your receiving another penny for it). The contract should be able to be terminated if the publisher is in breach of its terms (unless that breach is unavoidable) or if the book is out of print. Publishers have different definitions of what they consider out of print: on the whole, if no copies have been on sale in the last year or 18 months, you should have the right to request, in writing, that the publishers reprint the book and that if they do not do so within 6 to 9 months from the date of your letter requesting them to do so, you should be able to reclaim the rights. Something along these lines should be in the contract.

You should think very carefully before granting the publisher an option on your next book, otherwise you could find yourself under an obligation which you might regret.

payment
All the financial details will be set out in your contract.

What a writer is initially offered is an advance against the first hardback print run. This is based on the amount of money you will receive from each copy of the book sold — the royalty. Royalties can vary from 5 per cent to, perhaps, 15 per cent. Assuming that yours is 10 per cent and that your book sells in the shops for £10, you will receive £1 from each copy. If the first print run is 5000, your advance should be around £5000. The advance will be paid to you before the book actually hits the shops — a normal way would be half the amount on signature of the contract and half on delivery of the script or on the first day of publication: very rarely will the whole sum be paid over in one lump.

Supposing that the original 5000 copies are sold out and that the publisher thinks it worthwhile to print a further 5000 hardback copies: you have already earned the £5000 paid to you as an advance and will now begin to earn royalties. These should be paid over to you either once or, preferably, twice a year. With your royalties, you will receive a statement showing how many copies have been sold.

Once one book has been published, you should find the whole business of publication of the next one simpler than your original submission.

writing fiction

In the realm of fiction, books are classified in 'genres'—for instance, romance, historical, thriller, science fiction—and, in today's market, have to show a particularly original approach. Although this is a side of publishing that will never be glutted, it needs a very strong plot to break into the bastion of the massive best-sellers. A complicated story does not necessarily mean an interesting one—the central characterisation is equally important. And whatever the background, setting and events are, make sure that there are no obvious factual errors.

There are no hard and fast rules about the length of a book, but an average novel is between 80,000 and 150,000 words, although blockbusters can easily run to 400,000. Anything less than 80,000 words will be counted as a 'novella'—a form of novel publishers are not keen on printing.

other writing

One of the hardest forms of fiction is the short story, although it may appear relatively easy. It needs a great deal of skill to manipulate characters, tension and action within a tight framework. It is also one of the most difficult to find a place for, and the fees are small. Most magazines and newspapers or journals that publish short stories find their authors amongst already established writers, and a publisher will rarely want to take on a collection of short stories as the first work of a new writer to be published.

If you feel this is your metier, watch out for short story competitions, which are becoming more frequent.

Even harder to get into print is poetry. Only a handful of publishers deal with poetry books and it is a long, disheartening process finding one that will accept your work. Try looking through magazines that do publish poetry and approach them. Local papers are sometimes willing to publish poems or articles if the theme has a local flavour.

Try a local publisher: a few books published on a more limited market may open the door to large things later. The buyer for any large local bookshop will be able to tell you about any publishers in the area.

The BBC and ITV accept stories, scripts and plays from outside contributors, and so do local radio stations. For TV serials, it is not necessary to write the entire serial before you submit it. A synopsis and sample episode are enough. Scripts should be typed with 'sound' down the centre of the page and 'action' down the right hand side. Remember to time the work carefully, and to allow for commercial breaks if you are writing for ITV.

sources of help and information

There are numerous books on the techniques of writing generally and for specific markets, and many courses intended to enable aspiring writers to do so better. If you want such help, consult your local library or ask one of the writers' associations for recommendations.

The various directories of publishers should be in public reference libraries.

The *Writers' and Artists' Yearbook*, published annually by A & C Black (1988 edition £5.95), includes a broadly classified index of journals and magazines and their subject matter. It has sections on writing for newspapers and magazines, writing books, writing for theatre, TV and radio, on art and design, photography, music, translations. Each section has a few paragraphs giving advice on that particular market—for instance, 'poetry publishing today' and 'marketing a play'—and lists publishers and agents and outlets, with addresses and names of directors or other personnel and a brief note of the coverage and requirements with, in some cases, an indication of payment rates. There are details of the various literary prizes and awards that are offered. One section deals thoroughly with the complexities of copyright (british and US), subsidiary rights and agreements, the law of libel. The yearbook also covers services and societies, information on books that may be of use to a freelance writer, the mechanics of word processors, proof reading, book production.

Various writers' associations are listed in the *W & A Yearbook*. There may be special enrolment conditions, such as being a published, or about-to-be-published, author.

The **Society of Authors** (84 Drayton Gardens, London SW10 9SB), which is an independent trade union, gives members individual legal and business advice on matters affecting their rights as authors, and advises on individual agreements. Amongst its 'quick guides' (free to members) is one on copyright. The Society has established specialist groups such as the educational writers' group and the children's writers' group.

The **Writers' Guild of Great Britain** (430 Edgware Road, London W2 1EH) a TUC-affiliated union, negotiates industrial agreements for its members. The Guild is recognised as the body representing film and theatre and television writers, and negotiates jointly with the Society of Authors in the area of radio and books.

The **Book Trust** (Book House, 45 East Hill, London SW18 2QZ) has information on prizes and competitions and courses for writers. Details are given to members in the quarterly journal *Book news*, and in the regularly updated *Guide to literary prizes, grants and awards*.

Writing is a lonely business. If possible, try to have some regularity in working hours: exclude other things and be firm with friends and the family, who think that because you are at home, they can interrupt you at any time or ask you to do tasks for them.

indexing

For indexing, unlike writing, you do not have to have a creative talent but you do need to be widely read, methodical and logical in your thinking, have a good eye for details and an innate ability to make information contained in books and periodicals easily retrievable. Indexers are mostly freelance; relatively few are directly employed by publishers.

The most successful indexers are subject-specialists in one or more fields. Specialist knowledge of the subject-matter of a publication is more important for an indexer than familiarity with the world of publishing. It is necessary to have a grasp of the subject in order to understand the vocabulary, and a standard of education to degree level is generally called for, especially for scientific and technical works, the law, medicine and the social sciences.

You will have to make contact with many publishers' editors to begin with, in order to find one to commission you. Until good relationships are built up with two or three publishers and you have established a reputation for reliability and competence, work is likely to be very spasmodic.

It is useful to have your own typewriter, but preferable to have a micro-computer or word processor, and a set of basic reference books, with a quiet room to work in.

Because an index cannot be done until all the text is set and the pages numbered, it usually has to be done under pressure and to a deadline. It is usual to charge by the hour, or by a lump sum, rather than by the number of entries or pages.

Joining the **Society of Indexers** (details from the membership secretary at 81 Church Road, London w7 3BH) will keep you in touch with other indexers, technological developments and current rates of pay, through its journal *The Indexer* and newsletters. The Society circulates annually to publishers a list of its members available for indexing, showing which members are on the Society's register. Admission to the register involves paying an application fee and submitting a recently compiled index for assessment by the Society.

craftwork

When making use of a creative manual talent, it is no good expecting to sell the work of your hands unless you have reached a high degree of skill and can produce to a consistent standard. In many cases, you will be competing with established professionals so, if you want to be taken seriously, you will have to aim to attain a similar standard and not to approach the work as a dabbler doing just for fun what is another person's basic livelihood.

Given a good and cooperative tutor and some application on your part, doing a course in your particular subject should enable you to bring yourself up from good amateur status to a near-professional level where you can confidently ask other people to pay for your products.

West Dean College is a residential centre where courses on a wide range of traditional arts and crafts are given for adults; beginners and experienced amateurs are taught up to the highest professional level. Short courses are arranged for weekends and for 5 or 7 days' duration, in a variety of subjects, graded for all levels of ability. No entry qualifications are required. The categories of short courses include antiques (care and repair), art (drawing and painting), basketry, book binding, calligraphy, glass engraving, jewellery and enamelling, photography, picture framing, pottery, printmaking, silversmithing, textiles (embroidery, design, lacemaking, spinning, weaving), soft furnishing and upholstery, woodworking including cabinet making, polishing, veneering. There is a two-week summer course on a selection of topics covered by the short courses. The college also runs courses of one or two years' duration on antique restoration (clocks, furniture, ceramics and porcelain) but these are to enable students to attain a professional standard for full-time work in museums. For details of courses, fees, accommodation, contact the office, West Dean College, Chichester, West Sussex PO18 0QZ (telephone 0243 63301).

The index of topics in the **National Institute of Adult Continuing Education**'s twice-yearly list of courses at residential colleges in England and Wales shows what courses there are on craft-related subjects, such as basketwork, calligraphy, glass engraving, patchwork, pottery, spinning and weaving. The lists cost £1.15 each from NIACE, 19B De Montfort Street, Leicester LE1 7GE.

For Scotland, a list of residential summer and other short courses in craft subjects can be obtained by writing to the crafts section of the Scottish Development Agency (Rosebery House, Haymarket Terrace, Edinburgh EH12 5EZ).

supplies

Some manual crafts require plenty of space for equipment or the work. You may need a greater variety and range of materials than when you were doing the work as a hobby. Without being needlessly extravagant, do not stint on the quality of materials you buy. (You can claim a tax allowance for items used wholly for business purposes.) Some equipment may be available second-hand — but check its condition carefully.

There are mail order suppliers specialising in materials for handicrafts. For instance, Fred Aldous Ltd, having started in 1886, now claims 'a century of service to the craftsman' and provides a full range of handicrafts supplies. The Aldous catalogue, listing over 650 entries, is available free from POB 135, 37 Lever Street, Manchester M60 1UX. It includes materials for jewellery making, basketry, all forms of needlecraft and embroidery, candlemaking, chair caning, lampshade making, enamelling, papercraft, patchwork, stones and beads, clay, pewter and other metalwork. Also in the Aldous catalogue are books and leaflets from various sources and manufacturers. Another established supplier is Dryad (POB 38, Northgates, Leicester LE1 9BU), whose goods are available through shops and specialist suppliers.

finding outlets

It would be useful to talk to as many people as possible who are doing the same type of work or are similarly freelance, to gain from their experiences and know-how.

Once you have achieved a high level of technical competence, you should aim to sell not only to customers' individual orders but through general outlets such as craft shops and market stalls, or from your own premises. Perhaps a building society office, a bookshop or a teashop, or a hotel in a holiday area, will allow you to have a small display of your wares in the shop or foyer or window. Try to ensure that the things are properly displayed and clearly identifiable as yours, with your name and address.

When you are making to sell generally, rather than to a specific order, keep a note of the time a particular piece of work has taken you, so that you can add a suitable amount to the cost of the materials when working out a price to charge. You will have to set an arbitrary value on your own time: a realistic one might price your work out of the ordinary buyer's reach. When estimating for a commissioned article, cost in your time as accurately as you can.

markets

The Women's Institutes' cooperative market scheme covers hand-made craftwork as well as prepared food and preserves, and is not restricted to WI members. The markets are held, usually for one morning a week, in towns and villages accessible to rural producers. The money from the sale of the goods goes back to the producer, less a commission of 10 or 15 per cent.

The WI markets are subject to the usual trading regulations, and goods are sold at reasonable prices according to the locality. Men and women who are not WI members may apply to become shareholders for 5p and can then sell their produce through the markets, provided it comes up to the high standard required. Some markets which do not normally sell crafts do so for a limited period before Christmas and Easter.

You can find out whether there is a WI market in your county, and get further information on markets, from the market adviser, **National Federation of Women's Institutes**, 39 Eccleston Street, London SW1W 9NT (send a stamped addressed envelope with your request).

The Craftsman's Directory, a booklet giving details of craft shows and fairs throughout the UK and listing organisations of interest to craftspeople, is published annually by Stephen and Jean Lance Publications (Brook House, Mint Street, Godalming, Surrey GU7 1HE); the 1988 directory costs £5.

selling

Without previous experience in selling your wares, it can be difficult to get going. You may need to adjust your approach to other people to allow for the different relationship of seller and buyer, amateur and professional, customer and agent. You will need perhaps to be a little tougher in your approach, while remaining aware of the other person's criteria and needs. When trying to get a retailer to buy your products to sell in his shop, remember that he needs to satisfy his eventual customer, not you.

When you go into a shop to sell, have a definite idea of the price you want for your products. The price you ask depends on whether your articles are going to be bought by the shop for resale, or sold for you on commission. If the latter, your figure should allow for the deduction.

Be attentive to the retailer's reactions, comments and advice. For instance, he may like your products but not be able to display them easily, or may want them wrapped. A simple display unit could set off the work attractively: say, a shelf or some dowelling rods or hooks on a board. Some handicrafts need no wrapping or labels, others are much improved when appropriately packaged and labelled. Packaging needs to be in keeping with the character of the handicraft, and may need to be transparent. A carefully hand-written label with the craftsman's name adds a personal touch.

Offer to give a demonstration of your skill at local meetings of social or art groups—not to earn money there but to publicise yourself, show how good you are and get commissions.

Another outlet, once you are good enough, would be to give classes yourself in your subject. This might help to pay for equipment you need, as well as spreading the word about your skill and enterprise. Glass engraving, jewellery making, book binding and suchlike could be taught at home to amateurs.

sources of help and advice

The **Crafts Council** (12 Waterloo Place, London SW1Y 4AU) administers the government grant allocated annually for the crafts in England and Wales. It provides grants, loans and bursaries to craftsmen, under various schemes, to help them maintain and improve their standards, become better known to the public and sell their work. It holds regular exhibitions of work by artist craftsmen at its Waterloo Place gallery and manages the Crafts Council shop at the Victoria and Albert Museum. An information service is available on full-time and residential courses, on craft shops and galleries and exhibitions. Amongst its publications is *Running a workshop* (£5.70 by post) which gives comprehensive practical advice for the self-employed maker, and the bi-monthly magazine *Crafts*.

The **Contemporary Applied Arts** (43 Earlham Street, London WC2H 9LD) is a national association, partly funded by the Crafts Council, with the aim of promoting the best in quality and design in british contemporary crafts. Its members include individual craftworkers, craft societies and guilds, students, and people with a general interest in crafts. Individual membership (£30 a year) is open to anyone but is aimed at professional artist-craftspeople. Exhibitions and a retail display at the Earlham Street crafts centre are selected from members' work.

The **regional arts associations** in England and Wales promote the crafts by supporting craft centres and touring craft exhibitions; some provide bursaries for artists and craftsmen. A list of regional arts associations is available from the Crafts Council in London, and details of each regional association's activities are distributed locally through libraries and information points.

The **Arts Council** (105 Piccadilly, London W1V 0AU) issues free a regularly updated list of the arts centres in Great Britain.

The **Wales Craft Council** (20 Severn Street, Welshpool, Powys SY21 7AD) provides opportunities for full-time craft, gift and textile producers working in the principality to develop both direct and trade sales. The WCC encourages the improvement of design, production and professional practices, giving advice to WCC members and providing a range of activities and services. These include trade fairs in Wales and elsewhere in the UK; direct sales events for members at prestige sites in Wales; listing in an annual trade buyers' guide which is mailed world wide; an annual *Visit a craftsman* brochure listing workshops who welcome visitors and sell direct to the public; a database listing of all members for trade enquiries and special promotions. The application fee for membership of the WCC is £20 (1987/88), covering an inspection visit; then the annual registration fee is £42.

Support, advice and practical assistance for craftworkers is available in Scotland from **Craftpoint** (Beauly, Inverness-shire IV4 7EH), the national agency with responsibility for the commercial development of the crafts industry in Scotland. It provides marketing advisory services to individual businesses on a one-to-one basis, also grant-aid for market investigation; publishes buyers' guides and regular business bulletins; maintains a library and information centre. On a regional basis, the **Highlands and Islands Development Board** business unit (at Craftpoint, Beauly) provides training advice, short courses and financial support to assist development of crafts and business skills. The crafts section of the **Scottish Development Agency** (Rosebery House, Haymarket Terrace, Edinburgh EH12 5EZ) covers other parts of Scotland, with grant schemes on a discretionary basis to stimulate high standards of design, crafts and business skills; publication of *Craftwork* magazine; maintenance of permanent and touring collections, a slide bank for reference. The **Scottish Craft Centre** (Acheson House, 140 Canongate, Edinburgh EH8 8DD) is a contact point and has a display and retail sales outlet for members' work.

The **Rural Development Commission** promotes jobs in rural England. Rural Development's business section (formerly CoSIRA) at 141 Castle Street, Salisbury, Wiltshire SP1 3TP, can provide technical, business management and marketing advice to small country-based enterprises, and in certain cases can make loans to small manufacturing and servicing concerns, including crafts. It can only help part-timers where there is an expressed intention to build up to full-time work.

candle making

There are several ways of producing candles, some fairly simple, each giving different results. You can learn how to make the different kinds by buying a kit in a craft shop (rather expensive) and studying the instructions, or teaching yourself by trial and error with the help of books such as *Simple methods of candle manufacture* (£2.95 from Intermediate Technology Publications Ltd, 9 King Street, London WC2E 8HW).

In addition to wax, sterin, dyes, and wicks of the right size, you need moulds, either improvised or specially bought, a frame for dipping, vessels for the prepared wax. The process may be a bit messy until you are skilled, and takes up a fair amount of space for preparing vats of different colours, stacking the moulds or letting the candles hang while the wax solidifies.

The ingredients used carry a high fire risk; inform your insurers and be prepared for your premium to be increased. Be careful not to let the wax and sterin overheat when melting: it can flare up like overheated cooking fat. If you sell candles in candleholders, make sure that the candleholders are not made of a flammable material (plastic is not suitable).

glass engraving

For glass engraving you need considerable skill in drawing and designing. Talent as an artist is the first requirement; then a steady hand. If you make a mistake, you may have to begin again on another glass; it is expensive to have mistakes polished out.

A few further education colleges and institutes have courses on glass engraving, such as West Dean in Sussex.

The **Guild of Glass Engravers** (19 Portland Place, London W1N 4BH) is open to lay and craft members. Those practising engraving who wish to join as craft members and participate in the exhibitions organised by the Guild must be assessed by the Guild's admissions committee. The Guild's quarterly journal includes information about techniques and equipment.

Glass (or crystal) varies in quality according to the lead content:

the lower the lead content, the more difficult to engrave. But using hard glass may be more costly in the long run because it causes much faster wearing-out of tools, which are quite expensive.

Specialist suppliers of glass engraving equipment and glass include West Sussex Craft Supplies, The Glass Studio, West Pallant, Chichester, West Sussex PO19 1TD.

As well as allowing for your time and skill, your charges will have to vary according to whether you or your customer supplies the basic glass article. Ordinary glass may not be suitable for proper engraving. When glass is brought to you by a customer for engraving, you should insist on lead crystal.

A popular line is to engrave pieces of table glass with initials and/or dates for special anniversaries. Emblems for societies or pictures of houses may also be commissioned as gifts; these may need to be adapted for engraving techniques.

jewellery

The craft of jewellery is a varied one. At one extreme, it involves skills and knowledge which take years of practice to attain to a professional standard, and expensive materials such as platinum, gold and precious stones which are sometimes rare and often of very high value. Alternatively, the making of jewellery can be very simple, using low cost materials such as plastics, or non-precious metals such as copper, and may mean little more than sticking or stringing together bought components (called jewellery findings) and beads.

As well as simple basic handcraft skills, you will need to develop creative thinking and understanding of design. One way of acquiring this ability is to enrol for a local authority adult education course, preferably one leading to a City and Guilds certificate. There are also a number of other adult colleges, such as West Dean, which organise short courses from a few days to several weeks on specific subjects or techniques. Some private craftsmen open up their workshops to part-time students or short-stay visitors.

To establish a modest workshop and jewellery-making business at home will require buying quite a substantial amount of equipment and hand tools. A sturdy table or work bench is needed and tools for marking out, cutting and sawing, drilling, soldering and softening (annealing), bending and shaping, hammering, finishing and polishing.

Soldering and annealing require a suitable torch for the application of heat (up to 950°C). All the other processes can be done by hand, but are laborious; small machinery is available which is efficient and effective but is inevitably more costly in outlay than hand tools. Tools are a capital outlay and if seldom used, or bought only for one specific job, the cost can reduce or eliminate any profit on that work, unless taken into account at the beginning and costing stage.

The trade magazines are a useful source of information about equipment, suppliers and the jewellery trade generally.

hallmarking
Jewellery made in precious metals over certain weights has to be hallmarked if it is to be described and sold as platinum, gold or silver in this country. All work falling within the hallmarking regulations must be sent for assay and appropriate marking. The hallmarking law normally does not permit a piece to be hallmarked unless all parts of it are of the standards laid down in the law.

A summary of the hallmarking law, further details and current charges for registration and marking are available on request from any one of the four **assay offices** in the UK:

Goldsmiths' Hall, Gutter Lane, London EC2V 8AQ
Newhall Street, Birmingham B3 1SB
137 Portobello Street, Sheffield S1 4DR
9 Granton Road, Edinburgh EH5 3QJ.

The assay offices issue a free booklet on hallmarks.

You can apply by post for information about getting items hallmarked or go in person to an assay office to be told about the procedure for hallmarking and to get advice on specific or potential problems.

In order to have items hallmarked, you have to register your personal sponsor's mark with an assay office. The registration fee, which is valid for 10 years, is £46; in addition, you must have a punch made with a design showing your initials. The assay office will advise you about punch makers when you first enquire about registration.

For hallmarking, a scraping is taken from the article or components submitted, so it would be advisable to send the pieces in the unpolished state, to save time on the finishing when they are returned to you.

The complete hallmark consists of the sponsor's mark, the standard mark (denoting that the precious metal content of the alloy is not less than the appropriate standard), the mark of the assay office where the article has been tested (each has its own symbol) and the date letter for the year.

what to make
Jewellery can be complicated or simple, cheap or expensive, elegant or outrageous, and can be made of literally any material. The yardstick for the maker is to say: 'Is it good of its kind and would I buy it at that price?'

With inexpensive jewellery, you could produce a batch of work 'on spec'—for instance, if you are planning to sell your things off a craft market stall.

Where precious metals and gemstones are concerned, it may be sensible to produce a sample range from which orders can be taken. In this way, your work is sold before it is made and the financial return is assured. If you can persuade your customer to pay when ordering, perhaps by offering a small discount, you have your outlay costs paid and your profit in advance. But precious metals can fluctuate greatly in price from day to day and in the 'cash with order' situation, you must buy materials quickly, otherwise your calculated profit could turn to a nasty loss. So, you must keep up to date with variations in metal prices and, when quoting a price, include an appropriate disclaimer or set a time limit beyond which are you entitled to change the price. For special commissions or one-off pieces, always give an estimate rather than a firm quotation—this allows for variation in the final price which a quote does not.

Precious metals are usually bought from bullion dealers (mainly in London, Birmingham and Sheffield) and are supplied in sheet, wire, rod, tube or casting grain. The metal is priced mainly according to its weight and purity factor, but also carries a fashioning charge—for instance, wire tends to be more expensive than sheet because it goes through more production processes.

Beware: once you get known for buying silver or gold, burglars will become a constant threat, and you may not be able to get normal household insurance.

jewellery repairs
There is often a shortage of local people to undertake jewellery repairs, and the antique world is always looking for craftsmen to repair and improve objects on a regular basis, so there is plenty of earning potential in this field. But to do repairs requires a much higher level of knowledge and skill than making new jewellery.

One way of working and getting experience in this area is to buy, at markets or antique fairs, old broken and therefore cheap articles to practise on. This will quickly show you the pitfalls and problems, and test your skills and knowledge. If you do manage to achieve a good or at least respectable repair, you can sell it back into that market at an enhanced price. If, alternatively, you have messed it up, you have had the practice and learned from it. If you work in silver and fail to repair the article satisfactorily, you still have the scrap value of the metal to trade in.

You should never take on work which you are uncertain of being able to do or feel dubious about.

Examine all pieces thoroughly, if necessary through a magnifying glass or eye glass, for evidence of previous repair and use of any lead solder. This will appear grey in colour and soft when scratched. Use of this solder on precious metals is the sign of a bodged job: it will eat into the metal, usually with fatal results if re-heated. It is better to decline work that has previously been badly or inappropriately repaired. Remember also that very few gemstones will stand up to heat (i.e. soldering).

pottery

There is a market for pottery that is technically sound and has a little thought and imagination behind it to make it different. There are now so many good potters about (and some pretty poor ones) that the field is very competitive. If money is to be made, real quality is needed and the novice should aim at becoming a really good potter first.

Some personal instruction and consultation before buying equipment and setting up at home is essential. Do not go ahead and buy pottery equipment until you have attended a course or received advice from an instructor or talked with a professional potter, or at least studied some books on the subject—otherwise, you may find you have bought useless items. Even secondhand wheels are quite expensive. A wheel, however, is by no means a necessity. Some of the finest and most highly-priced work today is hand-built or modelled, and it is flair, originality and perseverance that lead to success.

An electric kiln is simplest for a beginner. A very small (3kW) kiln can be run off an ordinary household electricity supply: you can use it on the night-time economy tariff. A gas-fired or a wood kiln requires more experience and closer attention when firing, but more interesting results are likely to be obtained. With calor gas, you have the advantage of being able to put the kiln in an outhouse: a kiln makes the house very hot in the summer.

You can buy a variety of ready-mixed clays from potter's merchants; it is proportionately cheaper the more you order at a time, so as much floor area as possible for storing it will be useful. Clay keeps well in the heavy-duty polythene sacks it is sold in, stored in a cool place.

The chemicals used for making up glazes can be a health hazard, so wipe up any spilt powder immediately and avoid touching or breathing it. Similarly, dust from dried clay can cumulatively become a hazard: do not brush if off but wipe with a damp cloth and keep the atmosphere moist.

A simple guide to health and safety in pottery, with advice also on some of the more common problems that potters encounter, is given in the *Potter's Handbook*, available free from Potterycrafts Ltd, Campbell Road, Stoke-on-Trent ST4 4ET, who can also be asked to send their illustrated catalogue of materials and equipment for the craft potter, and their newsletter.

Perhaps you can use an outside shed or empty garage as your workroom but it should be cool and must have a sink and electric sockets. You will need a solid work surface and shelving.

If working in the home means limited space, the scale of pottery has to fit this. Small porcelain pieces can be made up with other simple materials, such as beads, wood and string to produce necklaces, bracelets, windchimes. Dolls' house crockery or dolls' teasets, little animals and ornaments sell for high prices, provided they are carefully made. Very little space is needed to produce this kind of work, and a sack of clay goes a long way.

In costing your work, allow for a high failure rate: with even a skilled potter, cracks sometimes appear during the firing.

If you join the **Craftsmen Potters Association** (William Blake House, Marshall Street, London W1V 1FD) as an associate or (if your work is of an acceptably high standard) as a full member, you can share information and interests with other potters, through the bi-monthly magazine *Ceramic Review*. Full members can exhibit and sell their work at William Blake House. The association publishes a directory of the work of full members, and has other publications and equipment available from its shop.

soft toys and dolls

To extend or perfect your technique, an adult education course on toymaking, puppet making, carpentry, pattern cutting and similar subjects may be useful; there is a City and Guilds certificate in toymaking.

When making toys by hand, you must be sure to make them safe, and suitable for the categories of children for whom they are intended.

Toys for sale in the UK have to conform to the Toys (Safety) Regulations 1974 (SI 1367; from HMSO, £1.40), the enforcement of which lies with the local authority. There is no active policing or

inspection of premises, but if a customer complains of a hazard, trading standards officers or environmental health officers have the right to prosecute if a dangerous toy—that is, one not conforming to the Regulations—is being made.

Current legislation refers to the British Standards Institution's *Code of safety requirements for children's toys and playthings* (BS 3443). Future legislation in the form of an EEC Directive is likely to be based on a revision of BS 5665 *Safety of toys*, part 1 of which covers mechanical and physical properties and part 2 flammability. The BSI has free leaflets of guidelines for the amateur toymaker, available from 2 Park Street, London W1A 2BS.

When making toys, you should ensure that eyes are well sewn in, no metal parts protrude, there are no sharp edges or spikes, that only non-toxic and non-flammable materials are used, that small solid particles and similar fillings for rattles are made of materials that will be harmless if accidentally swallowed, that any clockwork or driving mechanisms are enclosed so that moving parts cannot be touched, that any folding mechanisms incorporate a safety stop to protect fingers. Large toys intended to bear the weight of a child must stand level and firm in use, and also have no sharp edges, points or corners or unnecessary projections.

Stuffing materials should be non-flammable, new or disinfected, complying for cleanliness with BS 1425 (for example, materials intended for filling pillows have to comply with this standard). The stuffing materials should be non-poisonous, non-irritant and should not contain any hard or sharp foreign matter, and should comply with the Rag, Flock and Other Fillings Regulations 1981. Stuffing in the form of granules of 3mm or less in size should be enclosed in a separate internal casing within the toy.

If you want the assurance of a professional test, the BSI test house at Hemel Hempstead will test toys for eye security and flammability. You can telephone 0442-230442 to discuss what is required and ask what the fee for the tests and report will be.

Animals or dolls can be life-like or fantasy beings. If you invent a creature, you may be on to a best seller. But do not waste your time making existing television characters: these are copyright and can only be reproduced under licence.

Materials need not cost you much, but you will need space for your sewing machine, for cutting out, and to store bags of stuffing and other bulky materials.

Making—and putting on—clothes for dolls and animals is time-consuming but undressable toys are generally popular so you can charge extra for the extra time they take.

Dolls' clothes for specific sizes of dolls (choose ones which are widely sold) can be a good line to sell by post. Make them in pretty materials with a small pattern.

Another popular line, provided you have neat fingers and good eyesight, is dolls' house furniture, or even a complete dolls' house on commission. (Make sure the paints you use are non-toxic.) These can be collectors' items as much as toys and have to be of a very high standard of craftsmanship.

Whatever type of toy you make, the best selling time will be in the weeks leading up to Christmas. Make sure that you have a good supply then—even if it means that you have to borrow for the extra outlay. You may have to enlist helpers or outworkers temporarily.

new ventures

There are many money-making outlets for anyone who is energetic and organised, even without a previous skill or training, such as selling for others, keeping animals, looking after children. Choose something in which you have an interest and which you are likely to enjoy and therefore do well.

selling party organiser

A wide variety of products is sold through parties—jewellery, clothes, household equipment (Tupperware has always been sold in this way). A good way of getting a feel of the type of approach needed is to get yourself invited to one of these parties and, at the end of it, talk to the organiser.

A party organiser does not have to give all the parties herself but is expected to organise a certain number of parties a week which she has to persuade people to give. The organiser attends the parties to talk about and demonstrate the product and encourage orders. You are given an initial training course and usually have to be prepared to go along to refresher sessions to be kept up-to-date with latest products and developments.

You either get paid a commission of around 20 per cent of the cash value of sales from the firm supplying the goods or take the difference between the price the customer pays for the goods and what you have to pay the firm for them. Make sure you understand how the firm's commission or payment system works before signing anything when you are being taken on. Check whether there are any other incidentals, such as promotional leaflets, samples, or gifts for the hostess, which you may have to pay for.

Some paperwork, record keeping and accounting are involved. Finding alternative hostesses and potential buyers (not just good party-goers) is the most important part of the organiser's job. Generally, goods ordered at the party are delivered to the hostess and she collects and hands over the money for them.

The **Direct Selling Association** (44 Russell Square, London

WC1B 4JP) represents the direct selling industry. Most firms selling through party plan and other in-home selling systems belong, and there is a code of practice which members of the DSA are required to follow. A leaflet *Shopping at home* is available free from the DSA and includes a list of their member firms, some of which it would be appropriate to approach for in-home work.

telephone ordering agency

In some places, particularly in country areas, there is a demand for someone to take telephone messages or orders at home for firms. No capital outlay is involved (except for pencil and pad): the firm arranges for calls to be transferred during certain agreed times and you get paid for each call taken. The snag is that you may not get many calls to answer and be paid little. Look for advertisements in the local press from firms wanting this service—coal merchants, coach companies, carpet firms, upholsterers.

data preparation

Firms or organisations who send out questionnaires often need outside help to prepare the information on the returned questionnaires for computer processing. This work can be done as an outworker under instruction from an agent, without necessarily having previous experience. Training will or should be provided.

The work involves checking the content and continuity of the answers, sorting open-ended questions, adding coding references, and generally preparing the questionnaires for analysis by the computer.

You must be methodical, and will need adequate desk space, a large table and somewhere to store the questionnaires on which you are working. If they are not delivered and collected, the postage should be paid for you. The work is paid on an hourly basis or by consignment of questionnaires—which is more lucrative only if you are efficient and experienced.

You can try writing to firms in your area, but the most useful source is likely to be through previous experience and personal contact.

The **Market Research Society** (175 Oxford Street, London W1R 1TA) can provide a list of firms which carry out market and social research and which may offer work of this type for completion at home.

hiring out

It can be worthwhile investing in a stock of things that people need occasionally, in order to hire them out. Examples are bicycles, prams and pushchairs (especially in a holiday area), jigsaw puzzles, power tools, sewing machines, lawn mowers and other household or garden equipment. Build up on your stock when you find out what is suitable and popular, such as bikes with a child's seat, perhaps.

You must have good quality stuff, to stand up to being handled (probably often mishandled) by people to whom it does not belong and who may therefore be less than careful with it.

If you are lending something mechanical or electrical, such as a lawn mower or power tool, the machines must be kept in tiptop condition. It is as well to be able to do the maintenance and repairs yourself, otherwise your bill at the local repair shop or garage may eat up any proceeds from the hire charge.

Capital outlay may have to be high (six bicycles at one go) but you should get some immediate return. Your overheads involve mostly your own time on paperwork, and repairs. You must have a telephone to deal with enquiries and bookings.

You can set your own terms for length of hire, collection and delivery, charges for transport or postage, accessories or extras. It may be worth drawing up a formal hiring contract and getting it checked by a solicitor before putting it into operation.

Keep a careful record of who has hired what and when, due return dates, extras supplied (for instance, sander attachment), condition when taken. Ask for a deposit large enough to cover the cost of the article should it not be brought back or for the repairs if brought back damaged.

You are unlikely to be able to get insurance cover for the loss or damage of equipment while hired out. But you should arrange with your insurers for cover for the extra equipment and machines you have on your premises (there may be an extra fire risk from some) and for your responsibility in case anyone else or their property gets damaged through its use. The insurers will probably want to establish that any equipment (especially mechanical or electrical) will be regularly serviced and maintained in good order, and that you provide adequate instructions for its use.

Advertise in newsagents' shops, the local paper, at welfare clinics and, if you are in a holiday area, through the regional tourist board's publicity.

selling collectors' items

Someone who has enjoyed collecting as a hobby may find that his or her collection can become the basis for a money-making trade, given the right contacts and knowledge of the particular field of collectors' items: stamps, coins, specialist books, paintings, thimbles, matchbox or cigarette cases, postcards and so on.

The advantage is that a lot of the exchanging and selling can be done from home, by advertising in specialist publications, and by postal circularisation. You have to build up a list of potential sellers and potential buyers—a slow business. Postage will be the major expense. And you will need to be able to go out every so often to markets, auctions, shops, other dealers, to augment and replenish your stock.

boarding and keeping animals

Unless you live in a fairly isolated situation, this is a venture where you may run into trouble with the neighbours because of animal noises and smells. It would be wise to discuss your proposed arrangement in advance with your nearest neighbours, to get their agreement and cooperation.

boarding animals

If you board cats or dogs for payment, you count as the keeper of an animal boarding establishment and come under the Animal Boarding Establishments Act 1963. This means that you must have an annually renewable licence from your local authority. The fee for a licence to board animals varies with each local authority and may be as little as £15 a year or over £50. (The fees tend to go up each year, usually in April.) The application form and a notice giving details of the requirements are available from the local authority (generally the environmental health department).

Particulars required on the application form include the number, construction and size of quarters in which animals will be accommodated, heating and lighting arrangements, method of ventilation, water supply, fire precautions, arrangements for food storage and for disposal of excreta, isolation facilities for the prevention and control of infectious disease. An inspector from the local authority will come to check the proposed accommodation, arrangements and precautions. You will have to keep a register of the animals' arrivals and departures open to inspection by the local authority inspector or authorised veterinary surgeon at any time.

Anyone in Northern Ireland operating an animal boarding establishment, a riding establishment or a petshop has to be licensed by the Department of Agriculture. The Department's veterinary staff carry out periodic inspections of licensed establishments to check on the safety, health and welfare of animals kept there and to advise, where necessary.

It is worth taking advice from a veterinary surgeon from the earliest stage. Looking after someone's cat while the owner is away on holiday for a week is very different to having to look after a variety of animals, with which you may not have had any dealings before and may not therefore be able to recognise warning signals of illness or distress. Veterinary fees must be taken into account, as must the time commitment.

You would be wise to have an arrangement with a local veterinary surgeon to come to deal with any accidents or illnesses. This works both ways: a vet is often asked to recommend a cattery or kennels.

Amongst the publications issued by the **Royal Society for the Prevention of Cruelty to Animals** (Causeway, Horsham, Sussex RH12 1HG) is a series of booklets costing 25p which give advice and information about the care of various animals, including dogs and puppies, cats and kittens, guinea pigs, hamsters and gerbils, tortoises and terrapins, rabbits; also illustrated individual pet care guides costing £1.50 each.

insurance

Take out insurance for your liabilities. A block policy for boarding kennels and catteries, such as the one offered by the Equine and Livestock Insurance Company (Grove House, 551 London Road, Isleworth, Middlesex TW7 4EP), indemnifies you for legal liability to the owners of the animals (up to £250 per animal) and to third parties. The premium is calculated according to the number of animals you can board safely in your establishment.

A limited amount of cover is also provided for the owners while their animal is being boarded with you, but kennel proprietors are encouraged to get the owners to take out an annual policy ('Petguard' from Equine and Livestock) so that the owners would get a higher rate of compensation; the proprietor receives commission on any policy taken out through him or her.

premises

You will need planning permission from the local authority for change of use of your premises, and also if you intend to build any runs or pens for the animals.

If you are keeping the animals in pens or cages outside, there will be quite a lot of cleaning-out work to be done. It may be a good idea to have an extension bell for the telephone fixed outside the house, so that you hear it when out with the animals.

You have to decide whether you are willing to have any cat or dog in the house; if so, you would have to segregate incompatible boarders in different rooms or areas, which could be tricky.

Dogs will require exercising, not necessarily by taking them on walks, which is quite a responsibility. Provide an exercise area within your own ground where the dogs can be taken in turn a few times each day. You should not take on dogs unless you are an energetic person and like being frequently out of doors, regardless of the weather.

It is simpler to board small animals such as rabbits, gerbils, hamsters, caged birds and fish, which come in their own cages or aquaria. They can be kept in a suitable outbuilding: dry and draughtproof, with electricity if required for heating and aerating aquaria. Problems of compatibility or exercise do not arise and there is less possibility of cross-infection.

when taking the animals

Set a basic scale for boarding charges and make clear what they cover in the way of food and accommodation, veterinary attention, and what any extras will be. In some cases, you may want to ask for a deposit.

Your appointments system must be foolproof and accurate about bookings in and out and times for delivery and collection. This is particularly important during the holiday season, including the long weekends; be careful not to overbook. (You will have to time your own holidays so as not to miss out on the peak boarding times.)

At the time of booking, enquire when the animal was last vaccinated and against what diseases; ask the owner to bring vaccination certificates.

Find out whether a bitch is on heat or due to be. If so, you will have to be careful about taking male boarders at the same time, and will have to take precautions to keep neighbouring males away.

Never accept an animal with a hot nose, runny eyes, or any other obvious affliction. Ask for a vet's certificate of health if in any doubt.

Get all details about the pet and its idiosyncrasies (for instance about food) and any medicaments that may be required.

Make a note of any equipment that owners bring for their pets, and mark it with some form of identification. Ask the owner to provide brushes and combs. This is a saving for you, and minimises the risk of transferring fleas.

Record the animal's name carefully, and get the owner to tell you what commands it responds to.

Take the address or telephone number of where the owners are, or of a friend or relative to contact in case of emergency.

You may find that people call unexpectedly to have a look round, with a view to boarding their pet with you later, so try to keep the place looking orderly and welcoming at any reasonable time. A notice board beside the gate (for this, you may need advertisement consent) will help to guide prospective customers to your establishment.

quarantine kennels

Provided you have suitable accommodation, you could undertake to keep animals in quarantine for the period required by law: six months from the animal's arrival in this country.

Anti-rabies regulations apply to the importation of dogs, cats and other mammals such as rabbits, hamsters, guinea pigs.

Quarantine premises have to be authorised by the appropriate Ministry, and must be under veterinary control and supervision. There are high standards to be met and setting up such kennels can be an expensive business. To get Ministry authorisation, you must provide at least 10 compartments for the animals, you have to ensure strict supervision so that animals in quarantine have no contact with each other or other animals on your premises (this means segregated quarters and exercise runs, separate feeding and drinking utensils), and you must arrange for a veterinary surgeon (an MRCVS) approved by the Ministry to come to inspect the animals every day of the week.

Authorisation can be applied for in England to the Ministry of Agriculture, Fisheries and Food (MAFF, Hook Rise South, Tolworth, Surbiton, Surrey KT6 7NF), in Scotland to the Department of Agriculture and Fisheries for Scotland (DAFS, Chesser House, Gorgie Road, Edinburgh EH11 3AW), in Wales to the Welsh Office Agriculture Department (WOAD, Crown Buildings, Cathays Park, Cardiff CF1 3NQ). You will be sent detailed information about the standard requirements for the design, construction, operation and management of authorised quarantine premises.

For new quarantine premises, a scale plan of the proposed layout must be sent to the local divisional veterinary officer. (In addition, it will probably be necessary to obtain planning permission for the scheme from the local authority.) If approved, the work can be carried out but the premises must not be used to hold animals until inspected and written authorisation given.

Pre-exposure vaccination against rabies is available through the DHSS for proprietors and staff working at quarantine premises.

The authorisation of quarantine premises is annual for the first two years; thereafter, a re-authorisation review is done every two years. Premises will be visited regularly by a Ministry inspector;

if satisfactory standards are not maintained, authorisation may be withdrawn at any time.

A case history has to be kept of each animal, to be produced on demand to any official inspector of animals and kept for 12 months after the end of the quarantine period.

Although subject to Ministry control so far as your premises are concerned, you are free to charge what rates you choose, to cover the veterinary fees and extra care and responsibility that quarantine entails.

The animal's owner has to arrange for it to be met at the appropriate port or airport by an authorised carrying agent, who will bring the animal to your premises in a special enclosed container.

The owners may want to come to visit their pet during the quarantine period, so you have to be prepared to arrange visiting times and to cope with the upset the visits may cause the animals—and the owners. (Be alert for any kidnap attempt.)

When the six months' quarantine period is up, a release certificate is issued to the owner, who must then take the animal away from the quarantine premises.

rearing and keeping animals

Chickens, ducks, turkeys, geese, rabbits, goats, are possibilities to be reared for sale or kept for their produce.

Check first of all whether there are any restrictive covenants affecting your property that could be invoked to stop you keeping animals at all, let alone for any commercial purposes.

You may need to get planning permission for change of use of your premises, and certainly if you intend to put up any huts, sheds or other outbuildings.

Anyone keeping animals has to face up to the restriction their care imposes on holidays and time away from the premises. You need to be able to call on someone reliable to take over when you have to be away. An advertisement in a specialist magazine or the local paper might produce a suitable animal-sitter.

In livestock farming, the greatest single cost is feed, which typically accounts for between 60% and 70% of total costs. It is important to check the potential costs before being committed, and to establish beforehand that a market exists for the quality and quantity of produce you are planning to grow and the price likely to be received.

advice and information
Make contact with a veterinary surgeon whose advice you can ask and on whose services you can then call whenever the need arises.

The general welfare of animals is covered by the Protection of Animals Acts 1911 to 1954. Under the Agriculture (Miscellaneous Provisions) Act 1968, it is an offence to cause unnecessary pain or distress to livestock on agricultural land. In this connection, livestock means any creature kept for the production of food, wool, skin or fur; agricultural land includes land on which animals are kept for the purposes of a trade or business.

The Animal Health and Welfare Act 1984 covers the spread of disease, the slaughter of poultry, controls on breeding of livestock, animal feeding stuffs and veterinary drugs.

The Ministry of Agriculture, Fisheries and Food publishes many booklets and leaflets (some free) on different aspects of agriculture and horticulture. The livestock category includes poultry, goats, rabbits, bees. A catalogue of MAFF publications is available from Lion House, Willowburn Estate, Alnwick, Northumberland NE66 2PF.

The **Agricultural Development and Advisory Service** (ADAS) of the Ministry of Agriculture, Fisheries and Food produces a booklet *At the Farmer's Service*, which gives information on legislation, welfare of livestock, financial aid, and sources of further advice and help. There are ADAS centres in various parts of the country where specific advice can be obtained—look under 'ADAS' or 'MAFF' in the local telephone directory or contact MAFF at Great Westminster House, Horseferry Road, London SW1P 2AE.

In Scotland, a similar advisory service is provided through the three agricultural colleges of Scotland (the East in Edinburgh, the North in Aberdeen, the West in Auchincruive, Ayr).

The Department of Agriculture for Northern Ireland produces a booklet *At your service,* which includes an outline of the advisory and other services available to farmers and horticulturists in Northern Ireland, the addresses where further details of the various schemes and services can be obtained, and a list of the advisory leaflets available.

The bi-monthly magazine *Home Farm* (formerly *Practical Self-Sufficiency;* annual subscription £9, back numbers 60p to £1, from Broad Leys Publishing Company, Buriton House, Station Road, Newport, Saffron Walden, Essex CB11 3PL) contains useful articles about keeping various types of animals, giving practical suggestions about their care, accommodation, feeding, safety. The magazine also carries advertisements from suppliers of materials and equipment and foodstuffs, as well as hints from fellow 'farmers'.

The **Small Farmers' Association**, an organisation to encourage and promote family-worked farms and small holdings where most of the labour is supplied by the family, has a regular news page in *Home Farm.* (Further details of SFA from P.O. BOX 6, Ludlow, Shropshire SY8 1ZZ.)

poultry
In legislative terms, poultry means ducks, geese, guinea fowls, turkey and domestic fowls. Codes of recommendations for the welfare of livestock issued by MAFF and DAFS include one for domestic fowls and one for turkeys. You can ask your divisional or regional ADAS poultry adviser (in Scotland, a poultry adviser at one of the agricultural colleges) for advice on any problems you have with your birds.

Shelter from the elements, and at night, must be provided. To keep marauders, particularly foxes, from getting at your flock, you will have to put up protective wiring. For free range poultry, you will need plenty of land – at least 1 acre per 400 birds.

Where appropriate, and where suitable storage is available, it is usually cheaper to buy feedingstuff in bulk. Compound feeds, however, lose their palatability after a few weeks and it is unwise to buy more than 3 to 4 weeks' supply at a time. It is important to protect the feed from rodents.

The birds must have access to a constant supply of clean drinking water. Ducks and geese need a large area of grass (they will keep it short for you). All birds with access to roughage need insoluble grit (to assist the grinding action of their gizzards). Unless present in the ground to which the birds have access, it will need to be provided.

Newcastle disease and avian influenza (fowl plague) are highly infectious diseases of poultry. They are notifiable and, if you suspect either, you must inform the police or your local MAFF divisional veterinary officer. A veterinary inspector will come to examine the birds and, if disease is confirmed, will explain the procedures to be followed. A compulsory slaughter policy (with compensation) operates for fowl plague, and for the severest form of Newcastle disease. Less acute forms of Newcastle disease are controlled by vaccination and movement restrictions on and around infected premises.

If you are interested in exhibiting, the **Poultry Club** (secretary at Cliveden, Sandy Bank, Chipping, Preston, Lancs PR3 2GA) publishes a quarterly newsletter and a yearbook and also promotes the national championship show at the National Agricultural Centre at Stoneleigh.

The **British Poultry Federation** (52–54 High Holborn, London WC1V 6SX) can put you in touch with the relevant association for producers of table and laying poultry—chickens, hens, ducks, geese, turkeys.

hens and eggs

If you want the traditional pure breed hens, they will cost more to buy, and produce less, than the hybrid birds. Most types can be kept either in hen houses or on free range. You can charge more for eggs from free range birds (but they tend to lay less in the winter).

The time to buy is when the birds are within a couple of weeks of laying, at about 18 weeks old. Day-old chicks are cheaper but are tricky to rear. They need to have warm, dry, draught-free housing with a controllable temperature and good lighting. Even so, there will probably be some losses during the first few days.

Eggs—like all food sold for human consumption—must meet the general legislative requirements for food quality, hygiene and description. To comply with EEC regulations for the marketing of hens' eggs, a producer has to become registered as a packing station or sell only to a registered packing station. However, a small-scale producer of eggs on his own farm can take advantage of the exemption for eggs passed directly to the consumer, or sold in a local market or door-to-door. The eggs do not need to be packed or graded into the quality and weight categories required by regulations for hens' eggs sold otherwise. This means that you can sell eggs from your own premises (put up a notice at the gate) or through a local market. You will need a supply of trays or strong egg boxes; ask people to return them.

Ducks' eggs fetch more than hens' eggs. Some ducks are bred for egg laying and produce a steady supply throughout the year. There is no legislation specific to the sale of ducks' eggs but any eggs for sale must be clean. It is therefore important to have plenty of clean straw on floors where ducks lay, otherwise the eggs get badly stained and, with their more porous shell, there is a possible risk of salmonella.

table poultry

If you are not too squeamish to kill your birds yourself, the Slaughter of Poultry Act 1967 (extended by the Animal Health and Welfare Act 1984) lays down the permitted methods of killing birds.

Requirements to avoid mishandling poultry or inflicting any unnecessary pain or distress while awaiting slaughter and during the slaughtering process are set out in the Slaughter of Poultry (Humane Conditions) Regulations 1984.

You may have to have extra accommodation and equipment to meet the requirements for slaughtering and preparing birds for sale.

The Poultry Meat (Hygiene) Regulations 1976, as amended, apply to the preparation and sale of poultry meat. If you have had the birds for at least 21 days prior to slaughter, you will be exempt from the requirements of the specific hygiene regulations provided that you sell your slaughtered birds to the final consumer direct or at markets in your neighbourhood, or for direct consumption at restaurants, schools or other catering establishments, or to retailers in your neighbourhood who sell direct to the final consumer.

You must, however, comply with the Food Hygiene (General) Regulations 1970. The basic principle behind these regulations is the avoidance of cross-contamination and the possibility of subsequent food poisoning. These regulations, and also those covering poultry hygiene and welfare, are enforced by local authorities and you can contact your local environmental health officer for further information and guidance.

The Agricultural Development and Advisory Service of MAFF has leaflets on many aspects of poultry production, and an information pack for domestic poultrykeepers is available from ADAS Poultry Services, Government Buildings, Marston Road, Oxford OX3 0TP.

goats

Goats can be kept for milk production if you have sufficient space to provide them with a weatherproof shelter and a wired-in yard for exercise. Depending on their temperament, they can be housed together or it may be necessary to keep them in individual pens. Goats are adept at escaping and cannot be given the run of a garden or cultivated area: they would eat all green plants, trees and shrubs.

Like all ruminants, they require a diet made up of at least 40 per cent forage material—hay, grass, silage, clean vegetable waste. (Cabbage, cauliflower and carrots would be acceptable but some waste is poisonous: for example, potato tops, tomato leaves.) To give a high yield, the animals will also need a good cereal-based concentrate feed, such as dairy nuts.

Goats demand a high level of attention, seven days a week. It is therefore only possible to have a break from the routine if reliable relief help is available. At holiday times, arrangements must be made for their continued care and milking; otherwise, yields will drop and rarely improve later. Relief goat milkers are not as easy to find as for cows.

Goats are fairly healthy animals but, like all farm animals, may contract various diseases and would then incur high veterinary costs.

Foot-and-mouth disease is an acute infectious disease to which goats are susceptible. A suspected case must be reported immediately to the MAFF divisional veterinary officer, the local authority or the police. Affected animals must be slaughtered, and stringent precautionary restrictions are imposed on all premises for livestock in an area where an outbreak occurs.

The best way for most people to start up in goat keeping is to buy weaned female kids which can be mated as soon as they reach about 75 per cent mature weight. One goat can easily average 6 pints of milk per day. Small numbers, up to ten, could be hand-milked; milking machines are available for both small and large-scale enterprises.

Goats' milk can be sold raw and unpasteurised, but this makes it fairly fragile and limits its shelf life. Pasteurisation is possible and would be necessary for network distribution.

You can sell goats' milk privately or through a shop (in which case, your name and address and the word 'goat' must be on the packet or container). Although there are no statutory regulations controlling goat milk production, normal hygiene requirements must be met and a local environmental health officer may come to test the milk and milk products to see if they are fit for human consumption. Increasing amounts of goat products are sold through supermarkets, health shops and delicatessen. If the milk is made into a high-value product, such as cheese or yoghurt, it may be possible to derive a living from 50 to 75 goats.

Information on all aspects of goat keeping, particularly for the smaller scale goatkeeper, can be obtained from the public relations officer of the **British Goat Society** (Upper Mill Farm, Creswell, Worksop, Notts S80 4HF), together with details of membership of the Society.

Articles on various aspects of goat keeping appear regularly in the magazine *Smallholder* (published monthly by Chartered

Magazines, High Street, Stoke Ferry, King's Lynn, Norfolk PE33 9SF; 1987 subscription £15.50) and in *Home Farm*. The book *Commercial Goat Farming* by Katie Thear (£2.15 from the Broad Leys Publishing Company, Buriton House, Station Road, Newport, Saffron Walden, Essex CB11 3PL) is a useful guide, drawing attention to the various points that must be considered by anyone contemplating setting up a commercial goat unit.

There is a free MAFF publication on *Dairy goat keeping*.

The **Goat Producers Association of Great Britain** promotes commercial goat farming and provides technical and other information for producers. The secretary of the GPA is Mrs J B Barley, The Animal and Grassland Research Institute, Church Lane, Shinfield, Reading RG2 9AQ. The GPA's quarterly newsletter keeps members up-to-date with relevant information—for example, on publications, events and residential weekend courses on goat keeping.

For information about Angora goats (for mohair), contact the secretary of the **British Angora Goat Society**, Ash House, Iddesleigh, Winkleigh, Devon EX19 8SQ.

rabbits

There is a demand for good quality table rabbits, primarily from the continent where the supply does not meet the demand.

You can literally start with two rabbits and quickly build up to a herd of fifty or more (a doe can have six to eight litters a year). It is probably most appropriate to begin with a herd of about ten does and one buck. Buy the does when they are about 12 weeks old; bucks a month older.

The initial setting-up costs include hutching with well-constructed wire-mesh floors, or wire cages in a garden shed or garage; feed hoppers; wooden nest boxes. You need a way of supplying fresh water, and should feed the animals on rabbit pellets supplemented with a bit of hay.

Rabbits of acceptable weight and quality can be sold live to packers through regional collection points on a regular basis. Local butchers, too, are often willing to take live rabbits.

The **Commercial Rabbit Association** (secretary: Gauntlet

Chase, Sherfield English, Hants SO51 6JT) publishes a bi-monthly magazine for its members. An information pack (£5) on rabbit farming, including the code of practice and statutory leaflets, with a list of accredited breeders and market outlets, can be obtained from the secretary.

There are articles on rabbit farming in *Home Farm*, and MAFF publications are available on rabbit meat production.

keeping bees

Keeping bees is a specialist activity which can be a source of income from the sale of honey and beeswax. Bees require regular but not daily attention, and feeding with sugar syrup in the autumn, and occasionally at other times, particularly when the weather is bad.

You need properly equipped hives, a sound bee veil, a smoker and a certain amount of honey-extracting equipment and storage containers. The initial outlay is quite high, but do not be tempted to buy a secondhand hive unless you can be sure it is sound; it must be sterilised before being used.

The **British Beekeepers Association** offers advice for beginners or would-be beekeepers and will tell you about useful literature on the subject and give you the address of your nearest local beekeepers association. The BBKA publishes leaflets costing a few pence on, for example, swarm control, trees for bees, honey, and a free advisory leaflet *Would you like to keep bees* (all obtainable from the secretary of the BBKA, c/o National Agricultural Centre, Stoneleigh, Kenilworth, Warwicks CV8 2LZ; send a stamped addressed envelope).

The **International Bee Research Association** (18 North Road, Cardiff CF1 3DY) promotes the scientific study of bees; it publishes and distributes a wide range of publications, including the quarterly *Bee World*.

Most beekeepers associations publish local newsletters, and there are several nationally available magazines about bees and beekeeping.

There are a number of Ministry of Agriculture, Fisheries and Food leaflets on bees and beekeeping, such as advisory leaflet 283

Advice to intending beekeepers. (MAFF publications are obtainable from Lion House, Willowburn Estate, Alnwick, Northumberland NE66 2PF.)

Much useful material can be found in books such as *The illustrated encyclopedia of beekeeping*, edited by Morse and Hooper, published by Blandford Press (£19.95), *The beekeepers' manual* by Stephens-Potter, published by David and Charles (£8.95), *Beekeeping: a seasonal guide* by Brown, published by Batsford (£12.95).

There is an ADAS **national beekeeping unit** at MAFF's Luddington Experimental Horticulture Station (EHS, Stratford-on-Avon, Warwicks CV37 9SJ, and the national beekeeping specialist there can be asked for advice and guidance on all aspects of apiary management, including basic colony management for honey production, bee disease control, the rearing of queen bees.

honey and hive products

When honey is sold, it has to conform to standards for weight and presentation. There are composition and labelling regulations about honey (SI 1976/1832; from HMSO, 22p), prescribing definitions and descriptions for honey sold in the UK. Liquid honey is usually sold in net weights of 8oz, 12oz or 1 lb; you will need screwtop jars or plastic containers.

The old combs can be rendered down and the beeswax used or sold for making candles or furniture polish or cosmetic creams. These find a ready market and can be made at home at little capital cost.

Once established, you may find that there is a demand not only for hive products—honey, wax and propolis (a bee-collected resin used in varnishes)—but also for colonies of bees to pollinate agricultural and horticultural crops. The ADAS national beekeeping specialist at Luddington EHS can be asked for advice on where to obtain more detailed information and experience. The Hampshire College of Agriculture (Sparsholt, Winchester, SO21 2NF) runs regular courses on beekeeping and ancillary subjects such as hive building and accessories; the specialist course includes honey for sale, queen rearing, pollen identification.

looking after children

Do not venture into the world of looking after children unless you are energetic, healthy, adaptable and ingenious, have a high noise tolerance, and are not too houseproud.

childminding

Most of the children needing to be looked after are under-fives whose parents are at work. Before setting yourself up as a childminder on a regular basis, discuss the possibilities and what is involved with the local authority social worker.

Anyone receiving payment for looking after one or more children (not closely related to him or her), for more than two hours a day, has to register with the local authority social services department. This entails being visited at home, and providing the local authority with information about you and your premises and the care and facilities you are able to offer the children. You will be expected to have a safe, warm place for children to play, to have adequate kitchen and toilet facilities, to provide stimulating activities for them and take them out from time to time. Your health needs to be good; you will have to have a routine chest X-ray if you have not had one lately.

You may need to buy some extra equipment and playthings: cots, perhaps small chairs or stools, potties, playpen, building bricks and other robust toys that can be shared by the children.

Once registered with the local authority, the social services department will put you on their vacancy list and you can advertise yourself direct. The local authority may stipulate that you cannot look after more than, say, four children under five together (including your own). The health visitor or a social worker may call to see you and your home and the children. Some social services departments give practical help such as toy kits and other equipment on loan, and some run training courses for childminders. A few local authorities employ childminders direct.

A registered childminder is entitled to one-third of a pint of free milk a day for each child being minded. Claim forms are available from the area social worker.

Membership of the **National Childminding Association** (8 Masons Hill, Bromley, Kent BR2 9EY) costs £7 a year. The NCMA produces five times a year a magazine for members, *Who minds?*, and numerous publications, including a free leaflet *So you want to be a childminder*, a guide for childminders on *Tax and national insurance* (free to members), a childminders' handbook *How to survive as a childminder* (£1.75). It can also provide agreement forms to use when arranging a contract with parents and record forms to be completed by parents giving information about their child (both sets of forms cost 75p for a pack of 10). The NCMA has a block policy of public liability insurance for registered childminders who are members of the association.

There is no scale of charges laid down for childminding; in some areas, childminders have grouped together and agreed on a uniform rate. The National Childminding Association's guidelines on pay and conditions recommend 85p an hour (1987/88) as the minimum per child. You could charge more in certain circumstances—for providing extra meals, for example, or for keeping a child after 6pm, say, or at weekends.

You should stipulate payment in advance. Make clear at the outset whether you expect to receive holiday payment, either when the child is on holiday or when you are, and whether you will be paid if the child cannot come because of illness.

You should keep a register of when each child comes to you, together with basic information about his date of birth, address, doctor's name and telephone number, parents' whereabouts.

Ensure that you always know where to contact either or both parents, and when the child is going to be collected and by whom. Ask what the child can or cannot eat and any other essential factors, such as what the child calls the lavatory, when and for how long he sleeps during the day, what toy or other article is especially precious to him, warning signs of temper or tiredness.

A child who is ill should not be left with you. But you should alert your own general practitioner that you are childminding, in case you need his or her help for a child who is taken ill or gets hurt while with you.

You should have some basic knowledge of first aid and what to do in an emergency. The London borough of Hammersmith's health education department has produced a leaflet of hints for childminders on what action to take if certain symptoms or accidents occur, including what you should 'never' do (60p from Old Town Hall, Fulham Broadway, London SW6 1ET).

It would be sensible to get to know other childminders in the district so that you can group together and help each other out in times of illness or other emergencies or holidays. The NCMA has a booklet *How to start a group* (£1) giving basic hints on how to set up a group, with ideas for activities.

nursery group
Someone who is a qualified nursery nurse or has similar experience in looking after children could set up a private day nursery group for pre-school children. You would have to register with the local authority social services department and meet the local authority's requirements about accommodation, catering arrangements and staffing (particularly the ratio of adults to children).

The **British Association for Early Childhood Education** (Studio 3:2, 140 Tabernacle Street, London EC2A 4SD) can be asked for advice and information on running a nursery school, and has various pamphlets and booklets that could be useful (send a stamped addressed envelope).

If you prefer to start up a playgroup, which is based on parent involvement and not intended to make a profit for anyone, contact the **Pre-school Playgroups Association** (61-63 King's Cross Road, London WC1X 9LL) for advice and information, including the addresses of regional PPA offices. Amongst its publications is a broadsheet (80p by post) giving step-by-step advice on starting a playgroup.

taking lodgers

The size and layout of your house may enable you to take paying guests or lodgers. Before doing so, however, you ought to get in touch with the housing department of your local authority to check on their requirements for lodging establishments; some local authorities keep a register of what they call 'shared dwellings'. Ask whether planning permission is needed for the change of use or for any alterations you want to make to accommodate your lodgers.

If your house is rented, you need the landlord's permission to take in lodgers, and also for any different fixtures you want to install, such as gas rings or extra washbasins. If you have a mortgage on the house, you should tell the mortgagees that you want to take in lodgers.

If you have received an improvement or intermediate grant for work done to the house within the past five years, you may be required to repay to the local authority part or all of it when you change the manner in which you are using your dwelling from that shown on the grant certificate.

You have to advise your insurance company that you are taking in lodgers and you will automatically lose cover under your householder's policy for theft by someone who is on the premises legally, and for robbery without violent entry or exit from the premises. It is worth extending your insurance to cover your liability for injury or illness sustained by your lodgers and for damage that your negligence may cause to their property. You are not responsible for your lodgers' personal property, so you do not need to insure for its loss. But it would be fair to make it clear to your lodgers that if a thief who has broken in, or anyone else, steals their radio or any other item, it is their responsibility not yours to have insurance to cover the loss. With a larger establishment (say, of more than six bedrooms), you will need a special policy, designed for hotels and boarding houses·

When a householder does not have complete control over the occupants of the house, the fire risk increases significantly. Ask the fire prevention officer of your county fire brigade for advice on fire precautions to minimise the risk. Carrying out the fire prevention officer's recommendations may be expensive, but insurers may refuse to cover you unless you take the required fire precautions.

There is a Home Office guide to the Fire Precautions Act 1971 as it affects hotels and boarding houses (£2.30 from HMSO). Under this Act, you are legally obliged to obtain a fire certificate, from the local fire authority, for premises where accommodation is provided for more than six people (staff and guests) and some of the sleeping accommodation is above the first floor or below the ground floor.

It would be wise to ask the local citizens advice bureau or a solicitor about the terms on which you let rooms in your house.

The Rent Act affords a lot of protection to tenants, but holiday lettings are outside the legislation and so are arrangements where some services are provided—such as breakfast or other meals, laundry, cleaning. If you want to let rooms without providing meals, your tenants will have the protection of the Rent Act to some extent even when you are also living on the premises. The Consumer Publication *Renting and letting* includes information on the legal position of taking lodgers.

There are Department of the Environment housing booklets (for example, No 4 *Letting rooms in your home*, No 3 *The Rent Acts and you*) which give information about legal aspects. DoE booklets are free, and are generally obtainable at citizens advice bureaux and housing advice centres. The corresponding leaflets for Scotland can be obtained from the Scottish Development Department, St Andrew's House, Edinburgh EH1 3DD.

There is a City and Guilds certificate course in guesthouse and small establishment management for practising and potential owners, and also City and Guilds courses in professional catering and in food and beverage service.

getting lodgers
To begin with, it would be sensible to take people on a short-term basis: students, visiting teachers or lecturers, research graduates, industrial personnel on training courses, apprentices, holiday

makers, and such like. Get in touch with the personnel or accommodation officer of any nearby establishment where people are likely to come temporarily: university or technical college, manufacturing or computer firm, hospital, teacher or other training college, language school, repertory theatre. Someone from the organisation may want to come to interview you and inspect the accommodation you are offering. This contact means that you have some third party to refer to if there is any difficulty or disagreement between you and the lodger.

Alternatively, you can advertise direct, through the local paper or newsagents' boards, or just put up a sign at your own door (check with the local authority about advertisement control consent for this first).

The tourist boards have a free voluntary registration scheme for establishments providing accommodation. Registration leads to participation in tourist board promotions and in promotions run by many local authorities. One of the conditions of registration is that full, accurate details of the facilities and services offered are supplied periodically to the appropriate tourist board. Once registered, you can apply for the tourist board's classification or grading (the 'crown' symbol in England, Wales and Scotland, stars and letters in Northern Ireland), based on the facilities provided. There is a fee for classification, renewable annually. The accommodation will be checked by an inspector from the tourist board to ensure that it complies with the required standards. Brochures explaining the various grades and criteria, and application forms, are available from the national boards:

English Tourist Board, Thames Tower, Black's Road, London W6 9EL

Scottish Tourist Board, 23 Ravelston Terrace, Edinburgh EH4 3EU

Wales Tourist Board, Brunel House, 2 Fitzalan Road, Cardiff CF2 1UY

Northern Ireland Tourist Board, River House, 48 High Street, Belfast BT1 2DS.

In Northern Ireland, it is illegal to provide accommodation for the general public without being registered with the Tourist

Board, whose staff will inspect the premises. Various grants are available for the improvement of establishments providing overnight accommodation. Details of the grants scheme can be obtained from the Northern Ireland Tourist Board.

The **Wales Tourist Board** publishes a series of advisory leaflets on, for example, receiving guests, suppliers of catering equipment, advertising, charging, sources of finance; also a guide *So you want to own a small hotel*.

The **English Tourist Board** has a development guide (DG28) *Starting a bed and breakfast or guesthouse business* covering legal and tax requirements, financial implications, sources of further information, including other relevant development guides (£3 from the English Tourist Board, Department D, 4 Bromells Road, Clapham Common, London SW4 0BJ).

The **Rural Development Commission** has tourism consultants who are able to give advice on providing overnight accommodation for visitors in the rural development areas of England. Rural Development can also in some instances arrange loans for property improvement or conversion in order to provide overnight accommodation. Further information may be obtained from Rural Development's business service (formally CoSIRA) at 141 Castle Street, Salisbury, Wilts SP1 3TP, or from one of their county offices.

costs and commitments

If you are taking casual visitors, as you may be doing in a holiday area, you would probably find having a microwave oven worth the money, and also a freezer so that you do not get caught with insufficient supplies for a last-minute arrival.

You will need good easily replaceable crockery, and a hot plate or heated trolley would make the exact timing for meals less critical. Towels, bedding and linen will be another major outlay; have non-iron or easy-care bed linen. An automatic washing machine would keep down laundry costs.

Someone should be in the house at all times, to receive unexpected calls or arrivals and to keep an eye on the place, its

contents and inhabitants. You may have to let visitors have a key to come in late in the evening, but keep a close check on how many keys are being used and by whom. You may have to be prepared to lay down rules about bringing in friends.

Try to calculate the overhead expenses, including extra wear and tear on furnishings and linen, as accurately as you can, so that you include a reasonable proportion in your overnight or weekly charges. Be clear about extras, such as early morning tea, clothes washing, late meals or drinks. It would cost less in lighting and heating to share sitting and dining room with the lodgers, but you may prefer to keep your own household separate. A coin-box telephone may save arguing about bills.

Depending on how committed you are willing to be, you can offer just breakfast, or an evening meal also or full board. Putting an electric kettle in the visitors' room enables them to make a cup of tea or coffee, provided you do not mind this in the bedroom.

Find out what other establishments in the neighbourhood are charging and adjust your own rates accordingly. You may decide to give an obviously superior service or deliberately ask less to attract custom. Decide whether to charge per room or per person and what to charge for a single person in a double room. It would be sensible to ask for a deposit or stipulate payment in advance from casual visitors.

The law requires that in an establishment with at least four bedrooms or eight beds to let, the maximum and minimum prices charged per night have to be displayed.

foreign students

Lodgings for foreign students or school children may be needed in your area, for those who come, perhaps through a local school or college or a specialist organisation, to study in this country for a short period. Some come for holiday courses of two to four weeks, some for a full three-month term. You are paid by the organisation, not the individual students. School children can be voracious or unruly, and problems of communication and discipline may occur, so make sure that you know where to reach the person in charge of the group at all times.

If you want to contact language schools who may have students needing acccommodation, you can get a list of members of the Association for Recognised English Language Teaching Establishments in Britain from ARELS-FELCO, 125 High Holborn, London WC1V 6QD. A leaflet produced by ARELS-FELCO and available free from language schools, *A foreign student in your home*, deals with practical aspects and some less tangible points such as homesickness. Some accommodation agencies in different parts of the country specialise in placing as paying guests adult foreigners who come for language courses.

Host families are expected to provide a comfortable single bedroom, breakfast and usually an evening meal, and to share the family sitting room and television. At weekends, all meals will have to be provided, even if lunch is only a snack or picnic. The student will want to speak english with you and your family, and to share in your daily activities as much as possible. If you take more than one student, you have to try to ensure that they speak only english when in your home.

In most cases, the students go to english lessons during the day (you may have to arrange to get them to and from where they are being taught) and evening activities may be organised for them as well. In others, the paying guest comes individually and will rely on you for entertainment and activities, in which case your rate of payment from the agency will be correspondingly higher.

TAKING STOCK

Every so often you should pause in whatever you are doing and take stock to check what effect your freelance activities are having on

- o your health and wellbeing, temper, attitude to others
- o your ability to enjoy what you are doing
- o your family or friends and their reactions
- o your home and its state of care or neglect
- o your bank balance.

After allowing for inevitable family rows, debts, domestic crises and personal problems, if there is always more on the debit than the credit side, consider whether to stop.

doing badly

Putting the whole operation into reverse includes informing your surviving customers, cancelling any standing advertisements, letting subscription and registration fees lapse, closing a business bank account if you had one. Cancel any special insurance policy or extension you had taken out because of your business activities. Tell the local authority where applicable, and get your rates put back to the domestic tariff.

Advertise any equipment that you want to get rid of, locally or in *Exchange and Mart*: check first what prices are being asked for similar secondhand goods.

Inform your inspector of taxes when you stop trading. And remember to allow for having to pay after the event for any tax due from your business takings. There are rules for setting off losses and for assessing tax for the closing years of a business, and the date you choose for the termination of your activities can make a difference to the tax for which you are liable. It may be worth while not stopping until a few days after the beginning of the tax year, to minimise any additional liabilities—always assuming that, when a venture is going so badly, it is feasible to carry on until a specific date.

what your tax bill is based on in closing years of business

your last-but-two tax year:	profit in your accounting year ending in the preceding tax year	*taxman's choice:* when you tell him that you have closed down your business, he can choose to base your tax bills for the last-but-two tax year and last-but-one tax year (but not just one of them) on the actual profit for each of these tax years. He will do this if it makes the total profits for the two years greater.
your last-but-one tax year:	profit in your accounting year ending in the preceding tax year	
last tax year you are in business:	actual profit in that tax year	no choice

(taken from the *Which? Tax-Saving Guide*)

If you are ceasing because you have run out of money and got into debt, you may decide on bankruptcy. This is a serious step to take. Before going ahead, go for advice to a citizens advice bureau or money advice centre who can give you detailed information about procedure and alternatives, such as an administration order whereby you make regular payments to the county court which are distributed pro rata by the court to your creditors.

doing well

One of the snags of success is that you may find yourself with more orders than you can fulfil to the same standard as your original. You are then faced with the tricky decision whether to cause resentment and loss of custom by refusing work or to risk the complications of taking on a colleague to share the work (and the proceeds) or employ someone either in your home or as an outworker.

There is a City and Guilds special certificate course on small firm organisation for those who want to start up and manage effectively a small business enterprise. And there is the Consumer Publication *Starting your own business*.

The **Rural Development Commission** promotes jobs in the villages and small towns of England. General advice and assistance on setting up, running or expanding a manufacturing or servicing business is available from Rural Development's 33 county offices. Its technical, business management and marketing consultants will provide specialist advice at a small fee. Rural Development's business service headquarters (formerly CoSIRA) are at 141 Castle Street, Salisbury, Wilts SP1 3TP.

employing others

The role of employer carries certain statutory responsibilities regarding tax, employer's liability insurance, conditions of work, contract of employment, national insurance.

Booklet NP15, available from DHSS offices and tax offices, is an employer's guide to national insurance contributions. Inland Revenue leaflet IR53 *Thinking of taking someone on?* gives an outline of the PAYE system for tax deductions and IR booklet P7 is a detailed guide to PAYE (also including national insurance contributions) for employers; both are available free from tax offices. Leaflet IR71 explains about the inspection of employers' records by an Inland Revenue officer.

Employees over pension age (60 for a woman, 65 for a man) are no longer liable to make national insurance contributions but you would not be saved from paying the employer's share. And you would still have to cope with their tax under the PAYE system.

Using people on a freelance basis, even if they are self-employed as far as the taxman is concerned, does not guarantee the employer (you) exemption from the responsibility to collect tax and national insurance.

Enlisting members of your own family simplifies the employment situation. You can arrange to recompense them in kind or at a level below the thresholds for tax and national insurance. Where a husband employs his wife, wife's earned income allowance can be claimed to set against her earnings for tax. The taxman will want some evidence that the wife actually does the work she is paid for and that she has received the money for it. But where it is the wife who runs the business and her husband works for her, no extra tax allowance can be claimed.

In addition to tax and national insurance responsibilities, an employer is obliged by law to take out and maintain an approved insurance policy to cover liability for bodily injury or disease that an employee may suffer in the course of the employment. A short guide to the Employers' Liability (Compulsory Insurance) Act is available from the **Health and Safety Executive**, Baynards House, 1 Chepstow Place, London W2 4TF; also many other explanatory leaflets about health and safety aspects of employment.

Anyone you take on to work part-time for less than 16 hours a week is outside the employment protection legislation. If you employ someone to work for more hours a week, you must, in order to comply with the Employment Protection (Consolidation) Act 1978, give a written contract of employment after 13 weeks. After two years of working for you, an employee is eligible to claim compensation if you have to make him or her redundant or a dismissal is proved to have been unfair.

If you become a supplier for an outworker—who does for you typing, soft toymaking, assembling, finishing or whatever—you should do as you would be done by. The boot is then on the other foot.

making a business of it

If you are thinking of setting up a cooperative with any one or more like-minded individuals, to pool your skills and resources, it would be worth contacting the **National Cooperative Development Agency** (Broadmead House, 21 Panton Street, London SW1Y 4DR; telephone 01-839 2988) who can provide information about the different types of cooperative enterprises, advice on how to set up an appropriate cooperative, a registration service, training and support for cooperators, introduction to a local cooperative development agency. The CDA produces priced publications, free registration packages and information papers.

You can contact the Department of Employment's **Small Firms Service** (SFS) by dialling 100 and asking for Freefone Enterprise, to get advice and information on any specific query about setting up a business. The SFS can provide a general booklet *Guide to enterprise*, giving information about government advice and support schemes and contact points for further information. SFS's other free publications include *Employing people, Starting your own business—the practical steps, Running your own business—planning for success, Marketing*.

An information and advice service specifically for small enterprises also is provided

o in **Scotland** by the Small Business Division of the Scottish Development Agency, Rosebery House, Haymarket Terrace, Edinburgh EH12 5EZ

o in **Wales** by the Business Development Unit of the Welsh Development Agency, Small Firms Centre, 16 St David's House, Wood Street, Cardiff CF1 1ER.

o in **Northern Ireland** by the Local Enterprise Development Unit (the small business agency for Northern Ireland), LEDU House, Upper Galwally, Belfast BT8 4TB.

Each can provide individual counselling as well as numerous free publications and leaflets.

forming a company

If you decide to form a limited company, you will probably need help from a company registration agent or a solicitor or an accountant. Notes for guidance on company names and on incorporation of new companies are available in booklet form, free, from the **Companies Registration Office**, Companies House, Crown Way, Maindy, Cardiff CF4 3UZ (for companies in Scotland, from the Registrar of Companies, 102 George Street, Edinburgh EH2 3DJ).

The quickest, and probably the cheapest, way is to buy a ready-made limited company off the shelf, as it were, through a company registration agent (they are listed in the Yellow Pages telephone directory).

A company registration agent can supply a ready-made limited liability company (or will form a company specially for you) and provide all the necessary papers, books and the company seal. The agent's fee will be in the region of £125. To get a ready-made company, all you have to do is to complete an application form provided by the agent, giving the preferred name(s) you would like your company to have and other particulars about what your company is to do, the addresses and names of the proposed secretary and directors (there must be at least two), where the registered office is to be, what capital is available and the number of shares to be issued (minimum two). The agency puts the directorships and shares into the names of two people you do not know who will immediately resign once the company is incorporated, and the names of you and your nominees substituted. The whole process may take three or four weeks, depending on the pressure of work at the Companies Registration Office.

Northern Ireland operates its own entirely independent Companies Acts and all enquiries about a company to be registered there should be addressed to the Registrar, Companies Registry, Industrial Development Board House, 64 Chichester Street, Belfast BT1 4JX.

applying for a patent

If, deliberately or by chance, you find that you have invented some gadget or machine or method which is totally new and is capable of industrial or agricultural application, you may want to apply to patent it, in order to prevent exploitation of the same idea by others. It is essential to take steps to patent the idea before you disclose it to anyone (other than a patent agent).

The procedure for obtaining a patent is fairly complicated, from filing the application (which protects your invention for one year) to publication and grant of the patent. Fees have to be paid at various stages: for example, on making the application, for a preliminary and for a substantive examination. *How to prepare a UK patent application*, giving detailed information on the procedure and conditions, is available free from the head of publicity, **The Patent Office**, Room 866, State House, 66-71 High Holborn, London WC1R 4TP, who can also supply an application form and list of current fees, and other explanatory leaflets.

There are patent agents who will deal with the whole procedure for a fee and can advise on all aspects of patenting or other forms of protection of manufactured goods. They are usually listed in the local Yellow Pages telephone directory. A list of all registered patent agents is kept at the Patent Office or you can buy a copy (1988 edition £2) from the **Chartered Institute of Patent Agents**, Staple Inn Buildings, London WC1V 7PZ, from whom free information booklets are available on, for example, *Inventions, patents and patent agents; Trade marks, registered trade marks and patent agents; Industrial designs, copyright and patent agents.*

A patent lasts for 20 years, provided you pay an annual renewal fee after the fifth year. Even if you are unable to use your invention to produce a gadget, machine or process yourself, you can exploit it by granting somebody else a licence to use it, or by selling the patent outright.

value added tax

Once the taxable turnover (the total you charge customers for goods and services supplied, not the net profit you may make) of your total business activities has exceeded certain thresholds, you are required to notify HM Customs and Excise and be registered for value added tax.

The threshold for 1987/88 is £7250 in any calendar quarter or £21,300 over the four quarters of the year. It is the person not the business who is registered, so if you are already registered for VAT and decide to start a business from home as well, this simply becomes an extension of the activities of your business and you will have to start accounting for VAT straightaway.

You can ask for advice on the procedure and timing for registration at the nearest VAT office of HM Customs and Excise (look in your local telephone directory). The VAT office can let you have a current copy of their notice 700 *The VAT Guide* and other notices relevant to your situation, and explanatory leaflets such as *Should I be registered for VAT?*

Once you are registered, you must account for VAT whenever you make a taxable supply. Supplies of most goods are taxable and are liable to VAT either at the standard rate, which is 15 per cent, or at the zero rate, which is nil. Some supplies are exempt from VAT; if you make only exempt supplies, you cannot be registered.

You have to charge value added tax (output tax) not only on all taxable goods you supply but on any taxable service for which you charge: for example, hairdressing, providing accommodation or catering, doing repairs, giving professional advice. You can charge your customers for the appropriate VAT either by including it in the total price or by showing it separately.

Even if most or all of the goods you deal in are zero-rated, you have to notify Customs and Excise when your turnover reaches the VAT threshold.

As a VAT-registered trader, you can claim back the VAT you have to pay on most goods and services supplied to you (input tax).

The Customs and Excise leaflet *The Ins and Outs of VAT* explains input and output tax.

Once you are VAT-registered, do not include as part of a claim for a tax allowance on business expenses any value added tax you have had to pay—you claim it back through the VAT system.

keeping records

You have to put your VAT registration number on all invoices and are required to keep special VAT records. The Customs and Excise leaflets *Keeping records and accounts* and *Filling in your VAT return* are brief guides for the registered trader. VAT returns have to be sent to the VAT Central Unit, Alexander House, 21 Victoria Avenue, Southend-on-Sea, Essex SS99 1AA, not to the local VAT office. Take a photocopy so that you can refer to your declaration should there be a query when the VAT man calls to check on your return.

VAT surveillance is strict and the penalties for non-compliance are severe. You are required by law to produce records and associated papers referring to your business at any time when requested to do so by a Customs and Excise officer. You must keep all your VAT records and accounts for six years.

You will probably be visited by a VAT officer within 18 months of being registered. After that, the interval between visits will vary depending on the size and complexity of your business. The Customs and Excise leaflet *Visits by VAT officers* sets out to explain why visits are made and what happens.

voluntary registration

Even when your taxable turnover is below the limit for obligatory registration, it could be worthwhile to be registered voluntarily because this would enable you to reclaim any VAT you have been charged on any purchase or expense in the course of your business—for example, the tax on petrol (your claim for this should tie up with your claim for tax allowance on your use of the car for business).

Before such registration is allowed, you will have to satisfy Customs and Excise that you have a genuine and continuing need for registration, and you will have to accept in advance certain conditions imposed on the registration. Once registered, however small your turnover, you will have to keep proper records for VAT, account for VAT you have charged and render regular VAT returns.

de-registration

After being registered for two years, if you expect your future annual taxable turnover—that is, the total value of all goods or services you supply—to be less than £20,300, you can ask the VAT office to cancel your registration.

You may also apply for de-registration if your taxable turnover has been less than the threshold for each of the preceding two years and is not expected to reach the threshold in the coming year. The local VAT office can let you have the explanatory leaflet about *Cancelling your registration*.

INDEX

some other CA publications

Approaching retirement
Children, parents and the law
Divorce: legal procedures and financial facts
Making the most of higher education
Renting and letting
Starting your own business
Taking your own case to court or tribunal
Understanding allergies
Understanding cancer
Understanding mental health
Understanding stress
What to do after an accident
What to do when someone dies
Wills and probate
The Which? software guide
Which? way to buy, sell and move house
Which? way to repair and restore furniture

CA publications are available from Consumers' Association, Castlemead, Gascoyne Way, Hertford SG14 1LH, and from booksellers.